Madonna Center

Madonna Center

pioneer Catholic social settlement

Mary Agnes Amberg

Loyola University Press   Chicago 60657

© 1976 Loyola University Press
Editor, George A. Lane, S.J.
Design and jacket, Mary Golon
Printed in the United States of America

Library of Congress Cataloging in Publication Data

Amberg, Mary Agnes, 1874-1962.
  Madonna Center: pioneer Catholic social settlement.

  1. Madonna Center.   2.   Social settlements—Illinois
—Chicago—History.   3.   Catholic Church—Charities—
Case studies.   I.   Title.
HV4196.C4A52   1976   362.8′4   76-25594
ISBN 0-8294-0250-0

To my father and mother,
To our coworkers and benefactors,
To those whom we serve, and
To all who have given of silver and self,
I dedicate this chronicle of our common
efforts at Madonna Center.

Contents

Preface

This chronicle is more than a digest of my scrapbook of news clippings. It has been written out of the
lives, the unselfish devotion, yes, the heart's blood
and soul's travail of countless helpers who move all
too briefly and anonymously through these pages. In-
spirers, encouragers, conservers of the faith of our
charges, they have passed on to their eternal reward
while handing on to those of us who remain the torch
to light Madonna Center farther along its way.

The first of these is my dear mother, Mrs. William
A. Amberg; and though she has fallen asleep in the
Lord after a long life of duty done, Madonna Center
still feels her abiding and dear presence. The book is
likewise deeply indebted to my dear father, William
A. Amberg, who like mother was one of Chicago's
pioneers and who always seconded her efforts, often
at considerable sacrifice.

It would almost require a chronicle by itself to
record adequately the saga of Father Edmund M.
Dunne, Madonna Center's first chaplain and spiritual
director. I should need to add an entire volume to
the Jesuit Relations in order to recite our obligation
to the Society of Jesus, its priests and scholastics
and students who sacrificed precious time that our
charges should become upstanding Americans and
strong Christians.

The names of our benefactors who were and are
very dear personal friends abide with me in loving
memory. There were my grandparents, Mr. and
Mrs. James Ward, through whom our family has
spanned over a century from the frontier post to the
great metropolis that Chicago is today. There were

Mr. and Mrs. David F. Bremner, Sr., whose faith in and aid to Madonna Center never faltered. Another gracious Chicago pioneer, Mrs. W. Lonergan, was one of our cofounders--like Mrs. Johanna Kelly, a valiant Christian woman. The late William J. Bogan gave unstintingly of himself and his teaching and administrative experience. Father Frederic Siedenburg, S.J., gave us the benefit of his advice both as priest and social expert.

There were also Jane Addams of Hull-House and Graham Taylor of Chicago Commons and Harriet Vittum of Northwestern University Settlement--all pioneers who differed widely from mother in their religious views but shared with her the heat and burden of helping the immigrant in a new land.

Last and certainly not least, there is my coresident of Madonna Center, my lifelong friend, Marie Plamondon. Without Marie this chronicle would never have been written for she saved every clipping concerning anything and everything that went on at Madonna Center. One day two years ago our mutual friend, Father John F. Quinn, S.J., looked over Marie's scrapbooks and decided that on the face of things our center was no longer an experiment but the pioneer Catholic social settlement in the United States. He felt that we had something to say, and I was delegated to say it.

Mary Agnes Amberg
October 1942

Father, Mother, and Chicago in the 1860's

1

Madonna Center was the pioneer Catholic social settlement in Chicago. For over forty years it assisted in a much needed service and welfare work among the Italian Americans of the city's near West Side. Before I begin to outline its immediate origins and because so much of it owes to my dear father and mother, I hope my reader will bear with me while I indulge the natural desire of briefly tracing our family's background. It appears to me that such a remembrance of things past might be of interest to my younger audience, for it seems well-nigh incredible to realize that while Chicago is now one of the great metropolises of the world, we can nevertheless through parents and grandparents reach back over a full century to the Chicago of the pioneers. There is another reason for this musing; it is an attempt to recapture for our older readers and preserve for our younger ones the memory of our loved ones and of a grand and gracious era that is gone.

My grandfather, John A. Amberg, had voyaged from Germany to America as an emigrant in 1840. He settled in Bowling Green, Virginia where he took out his first and second papers, and in 1845 married Margaret Hoefler. My father, William A. Amberg, was born in Bowling Green in 1847 and to the end of his life was intensely proud of having been a native-born Virginian. There was indeed about him the courtly grace of the old cavaliers, their legacy to their fellow citizens of the beautiful state of Virginia.

In his infancy my father was taken back to Bavaria by his parents. He remained there until 1851.

When father returned with his parents to the
United States after their visit to Germany he was
already a boy of four years. On their return to
America the family did not resettle in Virginia but
was lured westward by travelers' tales of the opportunities of the frontier. They journeyed onward
to Wisconsin, settling at Mineral Point. Father received his primary education in the local schools
there and later attended Sinsinawa Mound College
conducted by the Dominican order. After graduation
father returned to Mineral Point and became a clerk
in the local dry goods store which served Indians,
French-Canadian trappers, immigrant miners and
farmers from England, Germany, Ireland, and some
New Englanders who had settled in Wisconsin. Busy
as Mineral Point was, it was not busy enough to
satisfy my father. In 1865 at eighteen years of age
he journeyed south to Illinois and Chicago where he
easily secured employment with Culver, Page and
Hoyne, Stationers.

In 1865 Chicago was a vast shipping port. Its blue
waters were alive with sailboats and steamboats.
There was a vigorous freight and ship chandlery business. Thirty lighthouses lighted the wooded shores
of Lake Michigan. 1850 had been the height of the
passenger steamboat prosperity on the lakes. At that
time sixteen first-class steamers left Buffalo and
Cleveland twice a day. These were extremely elegant
ships; their passengers were as well fed as those on
an ocean liner. The vessels carried orchestras and
vaudeville entertainers and usually made the trip to
Chicago in four days. The building of railroad lines
from the eastern United States westward took most
of this lucrative passenger business away from the
steamboats, but there were still many in use in the
middle sixties, and there were still a few in use
when I was a young girl.

Because of its location at the head of the Mississippi
Valley, the city of Chicago was a natural magnet for
the steamship and railway lines as well as for venturesome people of all ages. The urge to move faster

The north side of Lake Street between Clark and LaSalle while being raised to the new grade, 1860. Culver, Page & Hoyne at extreme right. Courtesy Chicago Historical Society.

than anyone else was already becoming a character-istic of Chicagoans. Old ways and old methods were being tossed overboard by the energetic midwestern-ers. Business letters, for instance, were written with quill pen in indelible ink and were sanded before being passed to the office boy to dampen and place in the letterpress book, thus securing a facsimile copy before mailing. The flimsy tissues were the fore-runners of the modern carbon copy.

My father is best known to the business world as the inventor of the letter file for loose-leaf filing of business correspondence. As early as 1869 when he was only twenty-one, he received the original patent on the letter holder, file, and binder, with other patents following for improvements on the original device. The busy army of modern business filing clerks are indebted to my father for their release from the captivity of the slow and cumbersome let-terpress record book, and for their introduction to the fast and efficient method of flat-filing and vertical-indexing of business correspondence.

Father was one of the most many-faceted people
it was my good fortune ever to know. His personality
inclined to efficiency and thoroughness. He had a
discriminating talent for literature, art, and music,
and a strong strain of the mysticism characteristic
of people of Bavarian Catholic ancestry. To father
Chicago was not only a growing city of opportunity,
it also possessed an inspiring Catholic tradition.
Here lingered the spirits of the early Jesuit mission-
aries and the French Catholic explorers. Isaac
Jogues, S.J., and Charles Raymbault, S.J., had
preached the faith to the Indians on the shores of
Lake Superior as far back as 1641. In 1666 the Jesuit
Relations had recorded Father Allouez's note on the
copper deposits of Lake Superior. Father Marquette
had come down from Sault Ste. Marie. Jolliet and
LaSalle had set their stamp upon the early traditions
of the Mississippi Valley. With a businessman's in-
sight father often commended to his fellow Chicagoans
the wisdom of the Jesuits and the early explorers who
had made St. Ignace their base of operations. His
business had taken him up and down the lakes and
he could marvel at the early Jesuit explorers' sense
of direction and economy of transport. Finally,
father felt at home in Chicago because of its large
and growing Catholic population.

The Chicago of that day was perhaps more colorful and cosmopolitan than it has ever been before or
since. It welcomed all new immigrants wholehearted-
ly and put them to work, and citizens whose families
had been Chicagoans for two or three generations
enjoyed a lively social and business life here. One
such prosperous and upstanding citizen was James
Ward, of Scotch-Irish ancestry, who had married
Mary Hickson. Their only daughter, Sarah Agnes
Ward, became Mrs. William A. Amberg, my mother.

Mother had lost her own mother when she was
very young. Like many another young Catholic girl
of some position in Chicago, she was enrolled as a
pupil of the Religious of the Sacred Heart at their
academy on Taylor Street, a very fashionable section

of the city. And I may add as a comment on the shift-
ing nature of metropolitan neighborhoods that this
very select school for young ladies stood exactly
where the Jane Addams housing development now
stands. Mother often told me how going to school
and church in those days was quite an undertaking.
She was driven by her father or the family coachman
across the prairie to the academy on weekday mornings and to Holy Family Church on Sunday mornings.
Its Jesuit pastor was Father Damen, a monumental
explorer-sort of man of dynamic energy and apostolic
vision. Mother was impressed by his saintliness and
was never tired of relating the tale of how one night
the spirits of two dead children of an ailing woman
appeared to Father Damen to urge that he bring her
the last sacraments.

I was always glad that mother had decided to
marry my father instead of someone else, and that

Mr. and Mrs. William A. Amberg about the time of their wedding, 1869.

out of all the very beautiful and accomplished young ladies in the city he had chosen and courted and married her. In those days the businessmen dressed very formally in top hats, morning frock coats, and striped trousers, as I myself can recall, but they were no match for the handsome ship captains and their officers. The men who officered a lake passenger boat were as important in Chicago as admirals. There were songs or chanteys made up about the best of them, and when they wore their gold-trimmed blue uniforms ashore, the ordinary businessmen looked colorless by comparison.

When mother married father in 1869, my parents moved to their new home on Sheldon Street, not far from where Madonna Center is now. Our "lot" consisted of two city blocks, and was even then shaded by elms and maples already old. We had a veritable Coney Island sort of grounds, with formal and informal gardens, fountains, slides, swings, whirligigs, seesaws and what not, and our place soon became a Mecca for all the rich and poor children of the neighborhood. Two blocks away in one direction was the "Gold Coast" of that day, two blocks in the other were the homes of a more average income group. Father often told me he was glad they had lived on Sheldon Street before moving to the North Side in 1900, for it was in mother's dealings with the children who frequented our home and shared its privileges that he sensed her possession of a grand and rare talent, that of caring for the bodily and spiritual needs of little children while managing everything with a wonderful administrative ability.

Looking back, the chief characteristic I recall about my mother was her lively interest in everything. She had a singularly happy temperament. I remember alighting from the carriage with mother along the riverside after we had visited prominent friends and how we both enjoyed the motley everyday sights and sounds of the commerce along the river. For a dime or a quarter the colored quartet on any passenger vessel would blossom forth into all sorts

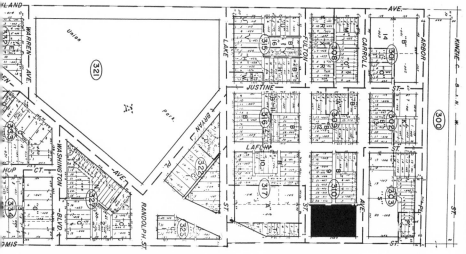

Sheldon Street (now Loomis) and Union Park area with Amberg
property shaded.

William A. Amberg home at 62 Sheldon Street, Chicago, in 1886.

of buck-and-wing steps and sing one of the few remaining lake chanteys.

It is not generally known that the lake sailors had their chanteys like those of the sea, though not quite alike. Many of the sailors came inland from the sea for the seven months of lake navigation, returning to the ocean during the winter months. One of the chanteys which father used to sing with comic dolefulness had a strange mixture of English, French-Canadian patois, and Scandinavian in its makeup.

A ship came sailing down Lake San Claire,
Shingle and cordwood her deckload were;
De win blew fresh and de win blew free
An sped her way dat "Look an See."
Out she sail from de creek of de Bear
Over de waters of Lake San Claire.

De win increase and she blew a gale,
De "Look an See" she reef her sail;
De water joop right over de boat
An way tree stick of cordwood float:
From gal to hurricane blow de win
Four bonch of shingle float behind.

Of course this chantey refers to a lumber cargo carried by lake schooners. The lumber traffic was very heavy in the early days of Chicago. It was a growing city and needed vast stores of building material. My father knew the captain whose boat freighted the lumber to Chicago for the erection of Old St. Mary's on lower Wabash Avenue.

The lake schooners had a peculiar extension of their fore-and-aft rigging which fascinated father no end. He had been accustomed to the square-rigged vessels which had brought him and his parents to this country. At the mastheads was rigged a triangular sail named the raffia, a lake-sailing development made necessary by the tremendous windstorms sailors now and then encountered on the lakes. A raffia sail enabled the schooner to claw off from the shore swiftly, thus saving lives and cargo.

It was very picturesque to see the river alive with shipping and watch the chanting and sweating steve-dores and sailors mending the sails with curved needle and palm-awl. They were a cosmopolitan lot: Scandinavians, French Canadians, Irish, and now and then one saw faces that were unmistakably full-blooded Indians. And they all were most formally polite to landlubber females like mother and me.

Life in early Chicago offered a very simple exis-tence for everybody. The society ladies contented themselves with visiting each other back and forth, paying stately social calls on New Year's Day, and administering households run on far more demanding schedules than we know today. Food was cheap and plentiful.

I remember how the butcher shops in winter would have frozen carcasses of bear and deer hanging out-side with festoons of prairie chicken, wild turkey, wild geese, and ducks. This venison and game was bought by the poor folk because it cost less than beef, mutton, and domesticated fowl! Lake Michigan swarmed with fish. In spring sturgeon meat was very cheap, as many sturgeon were caught in the Wisconsin rivers during the spring freshets. Smoke-houses everywhere sent forth the nose-titillating aroma of smoked sturgeon. Caviar au naturel crack-led in the frying pans of a morning for breakfast, and boys made grand baseballs by winding string around the rubbery snouts of the discarded sturgeon heads.

Early Chicago had its share of epidemics and the usual seasonal diseases for it did not have our im-proved sewage disposal. There were many minor plagues that set the stage for the great cholera epi-demic in 1873. Our medicaments were the usual pioneer and primitive ones. In grandmother's and mother's homemade pharmacopia you could find boneset herb for making a tisane considered good for malaria fever, rue for bad digestion, lobelia for minor fevers, butterfly weed for pleurisy, and the usual packets of tansy, camomile, saffron, wormwood, and other garden herbs. Many of the wealthy, though able to afford a family physician, usually kept Beach's American Practice on the marble-topped parlor table alongside the bible and the family album; and they prescribed, dosed, and I daresay healed as much minor illness as is done these days with specialists using hospital facilities. In winter a family might divide the store of navy beans into two lots, one to eat and one to make a poultice for cure of colds or pneumonia. Babies were born with the aid of female relations or midwives. Only the very well-to-do were confined to hospitals with physicians in attendance.

In the summer those who could afford to do so made the customary trek to Mackinac Island and other northern lake resorts. There the pleasures consisted of readying the house for its brief summer usefulness, dancing, lawn parties, and church. On Saturday afternoons the more "advanced" females went swimming, riding, or appeared at rowing clubs in suitable garb with appropriate nautical touches. I often wondered how mother and her friends rowed with the skirts and petticoats considered appropriate for such an outing.

The voyages up the lake to Mackinac Island were memorable in many ways. We saw the last of the famed lake craft called the Mackinacs which were fore-and-afters with almost square-rigged clipper efficiency. But for a time our yearly voyages were made upon some of the last grand passenger vessels of an earlier day. Because these were so truly luxurious and fast I hope the reader will bear with me while I recount a description of one of them.

The vessel was painted entirely white, and had a first and second cabin deck. The cabins were large and commodious with mahogany paneling inlaid with parquetry. The grand saloon situated on the main deck had a lofty roof line and was domed with stained glass. Here at tables laid with heavy linen damask, with cut glass and silver service, one was served

every luxury of land and sea for two dollars a day,
cabin included. There were usually five meals served
daily, two eight-course snacks supplementing the ample breakfast, dinner, and supper. Everyone who was
not seasick appeared for all five meals, and the men
invariably remained standing until all the ladies were
seated at table. From the main saloon the grand
staircase led to the upper deck. Tall torches con-
sisting of carved and painted Moorish chieftains with
spears held aloft with tinkling glass canopies of
Bohemian crystal shed light upon the deep-piled
crimson carpet. The staircase led up to a spacious

The passenger vessel Northwest, built in 1867, operated along the
west shore of Lake Michigan. Courtesy Chicago Historical Society.

observation deck whose main furnishings, aside from
the chairs, consisted of finely wrought brass cuspidors
which the tobacco chewers filled and the cabin boys
polished.

If a whole family like ourselves with servants and
young children was moving to its summer home, they
were not confined to the cramped quarters of the regular cabins. Besides the ordinary staterooms there
were several suites forward of the vessel finished in
white and mahogany with full-size beds of beautifully
carved walnut with overhanging Victorian canopies.
The beds had the most beautiful lace bedspreads I

have ever seen. There were even elegant lace cur-
tainettes at the portholes and large private bathrooms
with the very latest marble and brass fixtures. The
movement of the sidewheels and the soft endless
swish of the water lulled one to sleep in the summer.

If one delayed his return from the summer resort
until late in August or early September, the lake
usually got rough and one could get seasick far more
quickly and desperately than on the Atlantic Ocean.
It usually took only a day and a night to reach our
destination.

Time aboard the lake liners of that early day
passed magnificently. A well-chosen orchestra
played for square dances and slow waltzes every
evening in the grand saloon. The dance customarily
ended at midnight with a Virginia reel which invariably tipped over all the shining brass cuspidors
along the walls.

This was the easygoing pastoral social life in
Chicago up to the time of the great fire. The great
fire not only destroyed the beautiful frame homes of
the socially prominent and wealthy, it destroyed the
comfortable homes of others as well. The epochal
fire changed everything.

The Chicago Fire, 1871, and Reconstruction

2

Father's business had been prospering fairly well with the growth of Chicago. By 1871 Chicago was the fifth largest city in the United States. Its growth was so spectacular that everyone had all he could do to keep step with each day's expansion. It was hard for father to convince many of the more conservative businessmen, brought up with the old office methods, that they could improve their business and add to office efficiency with his office filing devices. Father kept a permanent exhibit booth in the Exposition Building at Adams Street and the lake and looked forward to erecting a factory of his own where he could manufacture his office filing devices. But factory space was at a premium. Business houses and dwellings were going up frightfully fast. The majority of the structures were made of wood because of its handiness and inexpensiveness. Father once told me that in 1870 on the eve of the great fire the lake traffic in structural lumber was at its peak. In that year 12,739 lake vessels arrived in Chicago with a total cargo tonnage of 3,049,265, mostly in unfinished lumber and cedar logs. The latter furnished paving blocks for the business section and the better residential areas. Most of the city's dwellings were built of wood. The bridges, docks, and piers were also of wood. The busy fleet of wooden schooners and steamers were tied up in the river. One can contemplate how a fire in such circumstances could soon become a frightful holocaust.

To meet such an emergency the city had a very modern fire department with regular firemen and volunteers who wore uniforms that made them the

pride of everyone. Men of prominence and social position did not consider it beneath themselves to be active
or honorary members of the fire patrols. It was their
duty and it was considered quite an honor and social
asset to belong to one of the patrols. The grand balls
and other social events staged by the fire patrols were
among the most impressive in the city and everyone
strove to be there. On the eve of the great fire there
were seventeen fire companies, fifty-four fire engines,
and four hook and ladder trucks that were municipally
owned. Besides these there were a number of engines,
fire, and ladder trucks owned by private volunteer
patrols. Such vast equipment, unusual for its day,
lulled everyone into a feeling of false security. And
furthermore, was there not a modern waterworks with
unlimited water from the river and Lake Michigan?

Father often remarked that the summer of 1871 was
very hot and dry, warmer and drier than any which
the old settlers remembered. For two and a half
months no rain had fallen in the Lake Michigan region.
The unusual number of Chicago fires and recurring
news of forest fires in Illinois, Wisconsin, and Michigan
should have been heralds of the unexpected disaster.
The smoke palls of these fires could be seen and felt in
Chicago itself. It added to the growing discomfort of
that strange summer. Even our own shady lawn on
Sheldon Street was parched for water and the super-
dry wooden floors and porches gave out a curiously
dull sound.

Then came catastrophe. A watchman keeping vigil
high in the cupola of the Court House that hot October
evening in 1871 spied a growing flicker of flame toward the southwest. He turned in an alarm and several
fire companies responded. But they could not control
the fire. Fanned by a rising wind from the southwest
the flames spread rapidly and within an hour it became necessary to turn in a general alarm.

The story of Chicago's great fire has been told and
retold so often that it is unnecessary to repeat the details here. But father's remark is worth recording,
that the preponderance of wood structures, board side-

walks, and cedar-block paved streets offered natural tinder for the spread of the flames. Even the substantial brick and stone buildings withered and twisted under the fury of those sheets of flame that seemed to come from everywhere. The dry hot air seemed like so much inflammable gas. As the general alarm spread and the bedlam with the city increased, father made sure his home was out of the path of the fire and then hurried down to his place of business, and with the employees who had already gathered there he strove to protect the premises or to salvage what merchandise he could. Most of it was office material and highly inflammable. Not much could be done. Expressmen were asking fifty to a hundred dollars to carry a load of household belongings a few blocks, and the problem of moving a business stock was nigh impossible.

The picture of beleagured people in flight is never comforting. The vandalism that quickly spread with the fire made any thought of moving the merchandise impossible. Fellow merchants had reported to father that their own goods, when loaded on express wagons for safe transport elsewhere, had been immediately followed by hoodlum gangs who pilfered and picked the wagon clean of merchandise before the conveyance had gone two blocks. In the face of the warning father stored as much of his merchandise as he could in the cellar below his place of business, secured tarpaulins, spread them over the floor, and wet them down with the assistance of his volunteer bucket brigade.

This done he left some trusted employees on guard and secured a buggy and rode home to assure himself of mother's safety and that of the house. The housekeeper informed him that my mother had gone with other neighboring women to Holy Family Church laden with blankets and food supplies in response to an urgent call from the Jesuit Fathers who had offered the church as a place of refuge for the homeless and terrified people who sought shelter in its vast brick-walled interior. The great church, which only that Sunday morning had housed an orderly congregation of worshipers at its many Masses, had now become God's hostel for the homeless. Afterwards as night began to fall over the hot horizon, father turned to alleviate distress as well as he could. He drove buggy load after buggy load across the bridge to the North Side until the bridges themselves became jammed and impassable from the quantity of broken down and abandoned vehicles. The yards and sidewalks along Michigan and Wabash Avenues had quickly become piled twenty to thirty feet high with household goods and other material abandoned by the frantic householders who had escaped from the fire and had fled toward what they hoped was the safety of the lakefront. But the high wind carried the flying embers, and the scarcity of fire-fighting equipment let the fire spread. Soon much of this distressed material, goods of the rich and the poor, was also in flames.

As the night wore on the terrors of the frightened people were increased by hordes of frightened cattle, sheep, and horses from the stockyards, and horses and cows from abandoned stables, who joined for safety in herds and stampeded blindly along the lakefront in search of water. A canopy of red smoke hung over the burning shipping of the river, with now a sail, now some rigging, disappearing upward into the smoke and flame. Along the wharves piles of lumber and hogsheads of tar, fat, and meat added stench to the flaming scene. For those refugees unable to reach the lakefront, the LaSalle Street tunnel proffered the only cool, safe haven; and it was crowded to each entrance.

Father said the great fire continued from Sunday afternoon to Tuesday morning when it burned itself out. Chicago cherishes its old water tower at the juncture of Chicago and Michigan Avenues because it is one of the few landmarks which remained after the holocaust. The entire lakefront area from Twelfth Street to Fullerton Avenue was burned down. Yet even as the fire burned itself out that fateful Tuesday, Chicagoans were already foraging in the charred ground for relics of the homes and business places

Fire of 1871. View looking north on Clark Street from the Court House. Chicago Avenue Water Tower at upper right. Courtesy Chicago Historical Society.

they knew. Already the telegraph wires were singing with incoming messages of hope and offers of help. The old Michigan Avenue Hotel at the southwest corner of Congress Street survived the flames and was taken over as a sort of "New Chicago" headquarters. Here father and other civic leaders quickly gathered to plan for the re-creation of the city they loved.

Although my father's place of business was located in the burned district, his precautions and prayers enabled him to salvage a good portion of his stock. Businessmen and chief clerks who had been too busy or disinterested to listen to father before now quickly began to introduce his office materials into their businesses. But I think what pleased father especially was the surge of human consideration that came to Chicago from everywhere in the wake of the great fire. Manufacturers and wholesalers magnanimously offered customers unlimited credit for needed merchandise and equipment. The English people undertook to replace Chicago's great library that had perished in the flames. Catholics permitted Protestant and Jewish congregations to use their places of worship until their own new buildings could be erected. Protestant and Jewish clergymen whose structures had survived the flames offered the same generous hospitality to Catholic pastors whose churches had gone up in flames.

In father's case, living expenses at the home on Sheldon Street were pared to the bone to permit him the utmost in money to meet the rapidly expanding credit needs of his business, now that the great fire had brought the name of Cameron & Amberg more prominence than ever.

The great fire had been more of a blessing than not in its effects. The rebuilt business structures and homes were more substantial than before. With all their old business records destroyed, businessmen secured father's new system.

The vast new program of building brought a new wave of immigrants into Chicago from everywhere. But the city was no longer using such enormous quantities of white and Norway pine from the lakeshores as it did before. The lake freighters began to suffer and their trade declined. Barges began to freight in stone and brick on the lake and via canal. Chicago was transshipping coal to growing manufacturing centers of the northwest via colliers and its mighty new web of expanding railroads. Steam propellers came into service along the canals aiding and cheapening water freight charges. The size of lake freight steamers was being increased faster than marine engineers thought correct but generally the new craft proved they were mistaken. About 1888 father noted the arrival of an entirely new type of freighter upon the lakes. They were more barges than anything else with a long hatch area amidships with the living and engineering accommodations forward and aft. Even in the seventies the Lake Superior region was providing great cargoes of copper and iron ore; but when the Mesabi Range was opened in 1892, the new barge-type steamers were absolutely necessary to freight the ore down the lakes to the smelters along the southern shore. Such ships, with a few steam passenger boats, now constitute all that is left of the vast commercial traffic of the lakes.

All this commerce and immigration had made Chicago a strange, Phoenix-like sort of metropolis, and father's business continued to prosper beyond his wildest imaginings. In that year (1892) he decided to retire, having established a subsidiary, the Amberg File and Index Company, which was to market his increasing number of patented office aids. Father felt that his son and associates could thenceforth carry on and that he had arrived at the age and financial position which demanded that he should give more fully of himself to the community. But the rapid success of the new concern soon necessitated the establishment of agencies in Boston, Philadelphia, Cleveland, New York, and London; and it was decided that none could make these preliminary contacts so well as father could. Besides he had founded the towns of Athelstane and Amberg in Wisconsin in 1887 to give the workers in the local granite industry a place to live. He had also founded the Loretto Iron Company in Loretto, Michigan. Whenever he returned to Chicago from visiting his far-flung branches, father busied himself with civic enterprises. Though not a politician or political leader, he was never far from the obligations of citizenship. He was also in the forefront in every Catholic activity. Our home was headquarters for all visiting priests on their way farther west. Yet even in the short space of time since he built our Sheldon Street house, the residential character of the city was changing. The well-to-do who had forsworn the lake and built as far away as possible from its salubrious shore, now seemed to realize the value of what they had left. The trend of better-class residences was toward Calumet, Prairie, and Michigan Avenues on the south, and later to State, Dearborn, Astor Street, and Michigan Avenue on the north. Father was busy with mother and consulting architects with a view to designing and erecting a new home on the North Side. This was completed in 1900, and father was once more free to devote himself to civic and religious activities.

Amberg home at 1301 North State Street, Chicago.

It is not only my own opinion but that of many others when I record that father was an eminently good citizen. Nothing that touched the welfare of his adopted city was foreign to him, and he ever stood ready to give of his time and finances without stint where a cause was worthwhile. He did not seek any public office, but much to his surprise in 1907 was appointed jury commissioner. In that position his native sense of right and justice helped him im-mensely and he brought to his work a keenly ana-lytical mind that could easily see through the most astute legal subterfuges. He vitalized his work and that of his associates and introduced a more modern approach to its problems, a factor I like to believe owed to his exposure to Toynbee Hall which he visited with mother on a London journey. Father took his position very seriously. In 1908 when father had gotten into his full stride as jury commissioner, Chicago had more inhabitants than Louisville, Jersey City, Indianapolis, St. Paul, Providence, Rochester, Kansas City, and Toledo combined. The Chicago banks held deposits of $698,335,473--almost three times the cash balance in the treasury of the United States. As the midwestern terminus of all the nation's railroads, Chicago had the largest car works in the world, had erected sixty-nine hospitals, and its business structures, theaters, churches, schools, and residences were rising and expanding on the grandest scale.

Father was glad when his term as jury commissioner was over, but found he had to continue by reason of a mandamus appointment to a second term. However, after his second term he resigned definitely, ending all active connection with the office. He wanted to devote more time and attention to the activities of his church. This was easy for a man of father's temperament, for, our church, in spite of some intransigence, was social minded in the best sense of the term. It established schools for the young and underprivileged, asylums, and hospitals. Nor was the intellectual side neglected. As early as 1888 father had been one of the founders of the Union Catholic Library Association. Mother rendered valuable assistance as auxiliary. Father later devoted much of his time and attention to the Columbus Club of Chicago which was a development and outgrowth of the Library Association. Unfortunately this club, which had been founded and fostered by outstanding laymen like my father, D. F. Bremner, Sr., Z. P. Brousseau, and others, met with discouraging apathy among the Catholic laity. This seems to have been a common fate of such lay ventures. Why this is I

William A. Amberg around 1907.

do not know. Perhaps it is not in the mass genius to sustain intellectual effort over a long period of time.

Later on father was among the laity and clergy who supported the Illinois Catholic Historical Society. He helped finance its publications and helped it become the valuable thing it is in the conserving of our Catholic cultural heritage in this area. And yet with all his interest in things Catholic, I hesitate to refer to father's charity, magnanimity, and social mindedness by any limiting denominational label. Whatever efforts our separated brethren were making toward the Christian ideal of citizenship, they always had his enthusiastic approval and support.

Of course mother knew this side of father's nature best, for besides rearing a family of three small children she had to be ready for unexpected extra guests. The family seldom sat down to meals alone. I think she looked for a respite when father's dear friend Bishop Foley died. Many of his young priests were accommodated at our house as a sort of way station when they returned from the seminaries and awaited parish or mission assignments. But after Bishop Foley came equally energetic Archbishop Feehan. And the flock of clerics, if anything, increased. Mother took it all in stride. In fact to me my father and mother were perfect Christian parents. Time after time I have heard from mother how Bishop Foley would tell father about mounting diocesan obligations. And I observed how it was with Archbishop Feehan. Their visits always resulted in a substantial check from father and his promise to enlist similar aid elsewhere. Nor were the needy immigrants overlooked. This aid to the immigrants took the direction of our incoming Italians. Holy Family, our original family parish, had a growing number of Italians settling on its eastern side.

3   The Pucciarellis Come to Forquer Street

There are parts of Chicago that are not Chicago. We often generalize about the city, thinking it is homogenous. The city becomes a cosmopolis because its population is made up of many diverse racial strains which mix and merge together. There are areas in Chicago where people continue to speak their native tongues and retain their national customs while remaining loyal to their new American citizenship.

Chicago was and is the microcosm and macrocosm, the epitome of natural and cultural resources, employer and employee, the native and the immigrant; the flux of diverse racial strains merge into the complete American citizen.

More even than the name of a city itself do its streets convey the spirit of a metropolis. London is Piccadilly and the Strand. New York is Times Square and Broadway. Chicago is the Loop and Halsted Street. This is fortunate for the one who searches through the jungle of a modern city for the resting place of its spirit. I do not think there is a parallel to Halsted Street in any other large city in the world. Somewhere along the twenty-two miles of this vast concourse you can hear the spoken language of every nation in the world. Hitler has not conquered Czechoslovakia nor Poland, for a vast segment of those people live and thrive along Halsted Street. For a space Halsted Street shelters our colored brothers, and you can see the setting for "Native Son" repeated several times over in every block. Farther to the south you find second- and third-generation Americans. But if you swing north again, you find Halsted Street bisecting Russian and Polish and Jewish neighborhoods where

some of the oldest Jewish-American settlers still
live and maintain their customs. There are prosperous Jewish businesses on Halsted near Twelfth Street
(now Roosevelt Road), and only a block or two south
is Maxwell Street. Many a Jewish immigrant has
graduated from a Maxwell Street barrow peddler to
a Roosevelt Road wholesale dry goods salesman, to
Lake Shore Drive, to a good business in the Loop.

Later on the Italian and Greek immigrants came
to Halsted Street, and they now dwell together in
peace in spite of the Italian majority. The Greek
shops offer lessons in sociology one could not easily
learn from a book. Not all Catholics care for squids
in stew on Fridays, or those gruesome sheep's heads
always leering at one from behind the windows of
Greek butcher shops.

The law of national motley continues on along
Halsted Street to the hobo hotels near Madison Street,
the lofts, warehouses, and factories of its river
areas, the German and Austrian section near Clybourn
Avenue, through more factory areas again and on
northward toward those typical two-flat red brick
fronts with neatly kept lawns and garages which have
come to be the symbol of comfortable middle-class
America.

Still later than any of the above came the Mexicans.
They had been inveigled from their sunny southland
by labor agents of the packers. The irony is that
they have to take sweatshop jobs in order that their
children may grow up in the American way.

The first group of Italian immigrants, a small
one, arrived in Chicago in 1852. Each successive
group of immigrants set to work to earn money to
bring over other relatives and friends. In 1892 a
violent and bloody revolt of Sicilian peasants and
sulphur miners broke out. Authorities claimed the
revolt had been ignited by the socialists, but our people told us that it also owed to low wages and intol-
erable living conditions. Pope Leo's encyclical
Rerum Novarum was read, the agitators were im-

prisoned and later pardoned, and relief measures promised; but the bulk of the population that could afford it emigrated to the cities of America. Employers needed cheap labor and lots of it for vast public works. As a result large numbers of immigrants who should have been diverted to the land were shepherded into the cities. The American bishops needed large congregations to finance and maintain the often too ambitiously planned parish projects.

In 1892 and thereafter in Chicago one thrust of Italian immigration centered on Forquer Street, near

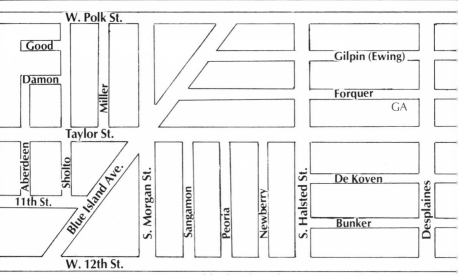

Forquer Street neighborhood on Chicago's West Side.

Halsted. Here was a harvest that cried aloud for some practical Christian. But except for some devoted clerics and lay people, few cared to listen. Some have asked why we of Madonna Center did not elect to serve the Negroes or the Mexicans. My honest answer to all such objectors was and is: We did not choose those whom we wished to serve. They were already there, a class of immigrants who needed us badly, and we undertook to serve them in whatever way we were able. It was all quite accidental--providential, if you wish.

Incoming population pressure and the fact that their limited educations ill fitted them for city life forced these Italian Americans to remain a low-income group. They had to band together, several families in one flat, to be able to pay any rent at all. The houses and apartments were never intended for such crowding. The area became a slum. To help illumine the injustice of such slum conditions, I beg the reader to visit with me the family of Tomaso Pucciarelli in Italy just before his family's departure for the great promised land of Chicago.

Tomaso and his wife Antonetta have for years cultivated a small farm some distance from their native village in the hills beyond Naples. There are forty families in this village, and each one has its little farm and vineyard located on the outskirts of the village. Even the priest has his own small podere which the other men give a look to now and then and keep cultivated when the priest has to be away. It is a simple pastoral life lived close to nature and close to God. And it promised to be so always until the day when the Pucciarelli's oldest son sent the stupendous money order from America. Their little Frankie had been in America only one year when he sent home a money order for 2,000 lira. This was a greater fortune than even the mayor of the village could accumulate in a lifetime and it immediately stamped the Pucciarellis as people of importance.

Francisco Pucciarelli, a vigorous young man of twenty-five, had emigrated to America two years before. He had written many letters to his family in a strange hand which meant that he had recourse to a professional letter writer. But he had secured a job as a roustabout in Chicago, had picked up a smattering of English, and eventually a persuasive labor agent on Canal Street had taken two dollars of his hard-earned money and sent Francisco up north to work in the woods. It was hard work, the air was cold, but the food was good and plentiful. Francisco taught himself to write and blossomed into a virile and handsome manhood. He was ripe for the persuasion of another labor agent who caught him before he had a chance to spend his lumberjack savings in the spring, and he was freighted with many other laborers to a railroad camp in Omaha. Here the pay continued good, the work hard, and the food excellent. Francisco did not care for the beer and whiskey popular among his fellow laborers. He did not draw his stake to spend in the saloons and bawdy houses of the great wild city of Omaha. He stayed on, became a straw boss, and graduated to becoming craneman on a steam shovel. Then in consultation with the padrone who was the interpreter for the Italian Americans in the railroad camp, he formulated a long letter to his family, in English in his very own handwriting. After expressing much anxiety for the welfare of his own Maria, his father and mother, his brothers and his sisters, his grandparents and godparents, and all their many kindred, he abruptly informed them that this 2,000 lira was simply the first installment of many that were to be used to bring the family and his adorata to America.

True to his word, the remittances continued to come from Francisco. And lest his family believe he was bewitched and the money was not come by honestly, his dear Maria soon had a tintype of her Francisco himself. He wore store clothes, there was a great gold watch chain draped across his carefully displayed waistcoat. He held a stiff bowler hat carelessly in one hand while the other fondled the tassels of a very luxurious portrait studio chair. All in all Francisco looked very grand, an authentic captain of industry.

The padre came to see the Pucciarelli family often these days as the remittances increased and his old friend Tomaso needed help in planning the journey. The godparents, overwhelmed that their godson should wish them to brave the Atlantic also, were making plans to dispose of their simple belongings and join the Pucciarellis. The tailors were called in and the seamstresses. Cheeses and salami were dried to help provision the voyage. The children were beside themselves with expectation and delight to be able to ride in a train and on a great ship. Maria Cirriaconi made a pilgrimage to the shrine of Our Lady of the Rock to beseech the blessing of God and the patronage of the Blessed Virgin for their new venture. She was Francisco's betrothed and adorata; and when she met him in Chicago, she would go to the beautiful church that he attended and become his wife.

There were many distractions to ease the anxiety of the Pucciarelli family. The weekly village dances were held more often at the homes of the Cirriaconis and the Pucciarellis. Friends and kindred came bearing gifts and victuals. Finally came the great morning to leave for Naples. Maria's prayers had been answered, the angels saw to it that it was a cool, sunny morning. They had all risen early and the padre had celebrated high Mass for them. The bishop had sent a special dispensation so little Martino, aged seven, could receive his first holy communion. Afterwards the padre accompanied his old friends to their home and bid them farewell and Godspeed.

The padre sat in the place of honor at the head of the table with Tomaso and his wife beside. Next to them were the grandparents, then the godparents, and the children, and Maria and the Cirriaconis, one by one, and so on down to cousins fourth removed. At another table, outside, sat the mayor and village dignitaries. The food had been cooked and brought ready to serve by the neighbor women. There was new wine. There was much laughter and banter calculated to hide grave faces, and merry eyes were bright with tears ready to well up beneath. Everyone knew something to tell about Tomaso and Antonetta and Maria and about the wild young Frankie who was doing so well in the new world.

But time and trains and ships wait for no one. An instant gravity fell upon the gathering as the mayor stood up and told of Signor Tomaso's neighborly and civic virtues and his value to the community. The spokesman for the other villagers recalled how their fellow citizen Signor Tomaso had been blessed by God with "green fingers" which made him very successful at aiding others to graft on to the vines their best shoots to improve the quantity and quality of the vineyard. The neighbors presented their humble gifts, a few firkins of cheese, the well-seasoned salami, small comforts for the wardrobe, toys to help the children pass the time on the voyage, a homemade tablecloth, and twelve natural linen napkins with insets of Neapolitan lace for Maria.

But presently the padre looked at his big silver watch, cleared his throat, and from his prayer book he read the prayer appointed by the church for those going on long journeys. When it was over he closed the book and his eyes and said his own prayer for his little flock that was about to begin its journey to a new sheepfold in a strange land.

When the padre finished his prayers his own eyes were wet. In a few minutes the glad and sad cavalcade began. The mayor rode in his carriage and the older people of the village walked with their friends and relations as far as the wayside shrine at the bend of the road. During the walk they all sang a hymn to the Blessed Virgin and St. Lucia. At the bend of the road the padre said a last prayer for the travelers, the older people left, and only the younger ones continued on with the emigrants.

I have written the composite story of an emigrant family from Italy in such detail to portray what was typical for most. What I most wish to convey to my readers, especially the younger ones who are native-born, is that America was peopled by just such daring, strong, independent, God-fearing people. America is the healthy country it is because our immigrants were not from blood-weakened, malaise-laiden noble or aristocratic stock. America was settled in the main by immigrants of sturdy stock, hardy and venturesome. It is the tragedy of the industrial era and occasionally of shortsighted shepherding that so many immigrants had to converge on the cities. This was the fate of our Italian Americans.

After Francisco, the oldest son, sent his savings to Italy to bring Maria and his family to America, he was beside himself with joy. Before this time Francisco's yearly schedule had been quite simple. He lived in railroad or other public works construction camps in the spring and summer, lumber camps in the fall and winter. It never occurred to him that it would be difficult to settle his family on one of the prosperous-looking farms he had seen, or that it would be well-nigh impossible to secure a homestead.

Much of Francisco's money had been spent to bring to America the most valuable resources it could acquire: alert-minded, law-abiding, healthy country people. Francisco had a fierce native pride which enabled him to hold his head high as his horizon began to narrow down from the coveted farm in the Wisconsin forest to the river-loam farm on the shore of the Mississippi to the tiny four-room "apartment" he had finally been forced to rent for his loved ones on Forquer Street in Chicago. The four-room flat had

A typical street scene on Chicago's West Side; Jefferson Street looking north from Twelfth Street around 1900.

originally been part of a rather proud residential mansion. There were three families living in it. The building already housed thirty people and the landlord was considering making two more apartments out of the attic.

Francisco had been driven to this by circumstances beyond his control. He spoke Italian well, but English with a marked accent. He had therefore been tagged as inferior. He was made to realize how much he differed from native Americans in diet, eating habits, amusements, drink, and even the way he wore his clothes. Francisco banded together with his own people for protection. If Maria's arrival and that of his parents and godparents and brothers and sisters meant the sudden destruction of all his grand dreams, at least he would be among his own. With Maria his native tongue and customs and kindred would sustain his ego.

Maria, the new mistress of the Pucciarelli household, had all the wifely virtues, the beauty and natural refinement, the poise and charm which are so necessary and desirable in a wife and mother. Furthermore she had the gift of loyalty, love, and a lively attachment to spiritual values. The nuptial Mass which had highlighted her wedding day had been a source of spiritual strength amid strangeness and fears. The Italian-American parish priest was there like the padre in the southern Italian village they had come from. He was not only a shepherd, but a counselor and a friend. And he had almost ten thousand like Maria and Francisco to shepherd.

The small cramped quarters which now housed Francisco and Maria, the parents, the godparents, and the brothers and sisters were a handicap from the beginning. Francisco no longer went so far afield for work, he did not make as much money, he was reduced to ditch digging, and he paid a large part of his wages as employment dues to a padrone. A resourceful firm of lawyers owned the tenement the Pucciarellis lived in. There were now five families in the building, and all used the same toilet with the

A one-room apartment occupied by a woman and five children on the near West Side.

cracked bowl off the landing on the second floor. In winter the Pucciarellis huddled around the stove. The landlord had not supplied storm windows nor panes for a broken sash, so they shivered and coughed. Because the building had settled on bad foundations, the floors were so warped that people stumbled when they walked about, and the children used the incline as a slide. There the family huddled and shivered, worried and existed, awaiting Francisco's return with his small day's pay. He had to work, for the Pucciarellis were a decent, upstanding family which had always paid its just debts and took no charity from anyone.

Maria was heavy with child by the spring and the godparents withdrew from the crowded household to make more room. This was a more sorrowful event than we may imagine, for Italians take the spiritual tie of godparents seriously. There was no extra money for a baby buggy, a picnic, a visit to the park by the lakeshore, no money for good clothes for the children, for natural food comforts for the old father and mother. Nor were luxuries looked for. With their native nobility these poor immigrants were looking to the new bambino's arrival as if it were the greatest blessing God had to bestow upon them.

I suppose at this point I could cite the teachings of Henry George to prove the injustice of what had happened to the once proud and happy Pucciarellis, and how the firm of shyster lawyers who were their landlords could have gained by giving the tenement quarters the merest hint of care and attention while drawing from it a greater rent than well-to-do families had to pay for a much larger and better house elsewhere. I should add that the firm of shyster lawyers was Italian, wily and wise as only shyster lawyers can be. But the exploitation of a race by its own kind is not strange or unusual.

And yet in spite of everything the Italian Americans on our near Southwest Side had a sort of native potential that kept them aggressively cheerful on the edge of this metropolitan jungle. Be it ever so squalid, when Francisco and Maria carried their bambino from their tenement and went out to sit and gossip with neighbors on a summer night, they glowed with pride. But when darkness fell upon Forquer Street a whole series of events on the gang's crime calendar came to life. From under the hot roof of the attic tenement came a baby's cry and the muffled sob of a mother who bent over the cradle as she rocked it and awaited her unemployed husband's return.

Mother and I sensed all this torment, and father also. I recall mother's rising revolt. To her it seemed not only tragic but diabolically ironical that strong working people of such proud lineage, excellent qualities, and high talent as these Italian Americans should have journeyed to the golden land of opportunity only to sink into the life of the slums. The majority of the Italian immigrants were not city folk but natural-born farmers. The Italian American instinctively preferred to work outside, grow his own food, and supply his own needs, rather than grub in the dark veins of the city for his money. With his deep attachment to the land he would have been a good help to the more erratic of the midwestern farmers. The Italian Americans withdrew into their ghetto neighborhoods and the city began to suck the joy and native exuberance out of them.

As if the jungle of tenements and privation were not enough, the two social settlements in the immediate neighborhood of Forquer Street were humanistic in essence. As our long time friend Graham Taylor or Jane Addams might have put it, they were "proving grounds for the social spirit." But they could be and in fact were dangerous to our Catholic Italian Americans who confused these "proving grounds of the social spirit" with the American way of life. Families like the Pucciarellis in their bleak despair might have confused such social outposts with the true American way and unwittingly sold their Roman Catholic birthright for a mess of proselytizers' and humanists' pottage. The archbishop and the clergy of Chicago sensed this danger. They were building schools and churches as fast as they were able to serve an immigrant population that should have been diverted to the land. But the lot of Italian Americans was such that without some providential outside assistance it was likely that the spirit of secularization would not only weaken the Italian American's Catholicism but cause him to fall away altogether.

4 The Beginning of Guardian Angel Mission, 1898

It was the summer of 1898. The annual retreat of the Alumnae Sodality of the Children of Mary in the Academy of the Sacred Heart on Taylor Street was drawing to a close. Father J. R. Rosswinkle, S.J., the retreat master, had placed considerable dramatic emphasis on the four last things, death, judgment, heaven, and hell. This morning the alumnae felt the exaltation of the righteous as they gathered for Mass and holy communion and the close of the retreat in the beautiful little chapel of the Madames of the Sacred Heart. They were prepared for the retreat master's final meditation, on heaven.

But the heaven which Father Rosswinkle pictured that morning was not the usual sort of heaven. Father Rosswinkle pointed out that heaven, if it were to be heaven at all, must be the very essence of unselfishness. The reason the rich man of Christ's parable had found it harder to enter the kingdom of heaven than a camel would find it to pass through the eye of a needle was not because his wealth in itself was sinful. It was his stewardship of his wealth which mattered, and he failed in that stewardship if his wealth was only focused upon himself. In proportion as he would extend his stewardship toward assisting his fellow humans, just so would his real self expand.

Of course the good old Jesuit was not as blunt as I have perhaps made him seem. But for a few days now these alumnae of the Academy of the Sacred Heart had been coming by carriage and cable car from all the better parts of Chicago to the fringe of the slum which was the Italian-American settlement around Forquer Street. Father Rosswinkle had known this ghetto life

at first hand. He had painted the slum canvas for his
retreatants in vivid slashes of life. Like a clarion
call he sounded for the Children of Mary the truth
that there can be no such thing as passive prayer,
prayer must result in spiritually productive action.

There were many notable early Chicagoans listening in the chapel that day. The list would read like an
1898 Who's Who. It will serve for the present to record
that at the instance of Father Rosswinkle and the retreatants, Miss Blanche Lonergan, Mrs. D. F.
Bremner, Sr., my aunt, and Mrs. William A. Amberg,
my mother, were appointed a committee to call upon
Archbishop Feehan and get his approval for a projected Sunday school to serve the Italian-American
colony in the neighborhood. The three women were
later received by Archbishop Feehan and were assured of his blessing on whatever efforts they would
make. And since a Sunday school needed a priest at
its head, Archbishop Feehan secured the promise of
Father Dunne of St. Columbkille's that he would be
the spiritual advisor. Thus did the bread which Father
Rosswinkle cast upon the waters return with the vast
spiritual increase of a spiritual director. But before
I fill in the new scene, I must endeavor to recreate
the background of this mission to the Italian-American
immigrants.

When the first Italian immigrants arrived in Chicago,
they had no church of their own but attended either the
Church of the Assumption on Illinois Street, St.
Wenceslaus (Bohemian) Church on Desplaines Street,
or Holy Family Church, a Jesuit parish on Twelfth
Street. In 1891 Father Paul Ponziglione, S.J., came
to Holy Family after forty years of missionary work
in the West. He busied himself with parish work
among the Italian immigrants and began classes for
the Italians at Holy Guardian Angel School at 711
Forquer Street in 1892.

Many have asked my mother and me why Guardian
Angel was chosen as the first name of the mission.
My mother named it from the school. She told me that
Father Ponziglione had told her that the name owed

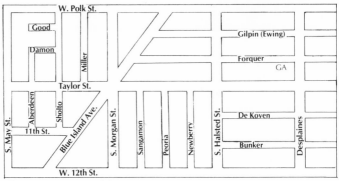

Forquer Street neighborhood.

directly to the first Catholic mission established in Chicago in 1696 by Reverend Francois Pinet, S.J., not far from the mouth of the Chicago River.

The Servite Fathers of the Church of the Assumption, intending to found a new parish in the area, had been celebrating Mass every Sunday in a large hall on Ewing Street near Desplaines. They were the pastors in 1898 when Father Rosswinkle urged upon the Children of Mary alumnae the need for a lay apostolate among the Italian Americans. The Italian community had been growing, but there was no organized catechetical instruction. The social venture would be pioneering of a sort for Catholic women because the typical well-to-do Catholic matron, while fully social-minded, belonged to a very conservative tradition.

Later on in this chronicle I pay small credit to our many friends among the clergy and the religious for their unselfish aid to our mission and its successor, Madonna Center. But at this stage of my narrative I must not go on without acquainting the reader with the personality of Father Ponziglione, founder of Holy Guardian Angel School on Forquer Street.

Born in 1818 at Chiascomo, one of the fashionable resorts of northern Italy, Father Ponziglione was descended from Italian royalty. His father was Count Felice Fererro Ponziglione de Borge d'Alea. His mother was Marchioness Ferrari de Castelnuovo. Like many others brought up in the lap of luxury, Father Ponziglione sensed the hollowness of it all

and decided to enter the Society of Jesus and study for
the priesthood. In 1848 while a scholastic at the Jesuit
College at Genoa, he was arrested and thrust into
prison by the revolutionaries, put in chains, and sent
aboard a man-of-war that flew the ensign of the King
of Sardinia. After a number of thrilling experiences
he escaped and succeeded in reaching Modena. There
he completed his theological studies and was ordained
a priest of the Society of Jesus.

He then offered himself for missionary work in
America. He was accepted and sent to Rome for additional preparation. But the anticlericals began to
stir up such hostile demonstrations that Father
Ponziglione had to flee for his life. His exodus took
him to Paris and into the midst of more violent anti-
clericalism. He finally reached the French coast
and secured passage to North America. On arrival
he was assigned to St. Xavier's College, Cincinnati,
and after a time was transferred to the Missouri
Province of the Society of Jesus where his missionary
activities began.

I wish I had the space to recount some of Father
Ponziglione's adventures among the Indians and the
pioneers of the far West. He was tall and hardy, his
face had the stamp of a man who would be a born
leader no matter what he did in life. He was a born
linguist and easily mastered the obscure dialects of
the Indian tribes among whom he worked. He neither
drank nor used tobacco. He was a pastor of souls
and a spiritual athlete. Likewise, though all his in-
clinations were toward the refinements of the cul-
tured, he never lost the common touch. In fact he
cultivated it. He was a delightful raconteur, especially of wilderness stories, which he could conclude
with a touch that would leave his listeners clutching
their chairs in horror. Though not a tobacco user, he
had once subjected himself to a tobacco-chewing con-
test with twelve Indian chiefs in order to attain a rank
equal to the medicine man of the tribe. Of all the
Indian tribes he was most closely attached to the

Navajos. He had a deep humility and a fiery affection and an interest in everyone, especially the Italians.

Men like Father Ponziglione were not only good Americans themselves, they gave generously of their time, training, knowledge, and education so that those less favored might become good Americans too. They were apostles of Christ and of Americanism. They taught their charges the new rules, the new speech, the new ways, while retaining a careful loyalty to the old.

It was sad, however, that the Italians arrived in America only to meet again the feudalism which they had tried to escape by emigrating. The padrone took them in hand. The padrone was of the same origin, as illiterate but more resourceful than the other immigrants. It is difficult to reconstruct for the non-Latin reader just the sort of functionary the padrone was, but it may assist the reader's imagination if he pictures him as a sort of alderman without portfolio. Even if he did not know all about English and education, he knew almost everything else.

When Francisco Pucciarelli arrived in America for the first time, it was the padrone's representative who met him and arranged for his journey to Chicago. He was the agent who sped Francisco to the huge construction projects of the railroads, who arranged for Francisco's sortie into the north woods in the fall and winter. Whenever Francisco ran afoul of the civil authorities, justifiably or not, the padrone arranged matters to the satisfaction of everyone, with the possible exception of Francisco. The padrone worked hand-in-glove with the ward boss and usually received an allowance for the delivery of immigrant votes en bloc at election time. The padrone knew everyone who was anyone, including those city brigands who were better off not known at all. He was the prime minister for rapacious landlords, the emissary of pitiless bailiffs. And in spite of all his asocial ferociousness, he occasionally found time to be good. For he was, if powerful enough, a sort of mayor in his area. He made matches, arranged betrothals, set likely prospects up in business, fought to give his people a sort of civic identity, and lived a very full life playing both immigrant ends against an American middle. The padrone ultimately failed because he was an opportunist first and a citizen afterward. Few ever attained the status of real men of affairs in their communities.

The social settlement's first reason for existence in any city was to be a social thrust against such unsocial or asocial gentry. The social settlement could have been a valuable adjunct of Catholic immigrant communities everywhere in America had there been fewer social intransigents among our clergy and laity and more pastors like Fathers Rosswinkle and Ponziglione, and more laity like my father and mother. Because there were not, some Protestant social settlements set themselves up under the very shadow of Catholic steeples. The Roman Catholic Church, in fact any Christian or Jewish denomination, is strategically able to dominate the social field. Our Church held and still holds a social gospel which, if not superior to, is certainly equal to that of any social-minded outsider. The pity was and is, that some of us, clerics and laity, too often fail to translate our gospel into all its social implications. So it was providential that mother and her helpers had the example and guidance of two such fine pastors as Father Rosswinkle and Father Ponziglione.

With my mother, deciding and doing were all but synonymous. I think it was this quality that caused the others of the retreat group to look on mother as a sort of dea ex machina. I daresay that Father Rosswinkle welcomed the committee. He was alert to the difficulties Father Ponziglione had encountered. The work of his fellow priest deserved assistance. If mother and her aides were really in earnest, Father Rosswinkle knew where their lay evangelism among the Italian Americans could begin. Holy Guardian Angel School belonged to the Society of Jesus; it was in disuse, and it was ideal for a mission.

Holy Guardian Angel School, 711 Forquer Street, opened in 1875.

In the spring of 1898 the Jesuits gave two rooms on the second floor of Holy Guardian Angel School to mother and her assistants. Mother immediately broadcast her needs to friends, acquaintances, and sundry citizens, clerical as well as lay. Mother's first acquisition was a picture of Our Lady of Perpetual Help. It was the first picture hung upon the walls. The building was dingy from many years of disuse. Quite a few lacy petticoats were pinned up for scrubbing the humble two-room site of the newly formed mission. Odds and ends of furniture were donated. At the end of the week the workers cried hysterically with joy and fatigue when they observed how they had transformed two classrooms into a liturgical chapel with completely equipped main and side altars with space enough to accommodate seventy-five worshipers. There were not enough pews at first, mother used to relate. The congregation stood and knelt, the women on one side of the chapel, the men on the other, old-country fashion.

The mission so far had no permanent spiritual director, but was served by first one and then another Jesuit priest of St. Ignatius College. Then one day a family friend, Father Edmund M. Dunne, a young curate at St. Columbkille's, rode over with mother to have a look at the mission. The Sunday school had begun with forty children and adults in attendance, had grown to seventy-five within a few weeks, and was expanding like a mushroom. Father Dunne was so impressed that he undertook to serve as pastor of the mission, and every Sunday, after saying the parish Mass at St. Columbkille's, he came over and said Mass for the Italian Americans at the Guardian Angel Mission.

Every Sunday before Mass mother and her helpers conducted the Sunday school. I should add that while the alumnae of the Academy of the Sacred Heart under-took to found the mission and support it, much of the actual work came from their daughters who attended the new Academy of the Sacred Heart in Lake Forest. For many of them it was an all-day journey to work at the mission.

At the outset the mission operated only on the funds donated by the founders. It began on a shoe-string. As Father Dunne came fasting to the mission on Sunday morning, and as collections were almost nil, mother saw to it that he had a nourishing dinner. Well do I remember the Sunday morning preparations at our home. If there was to be roast chicken for dinner, it had to be prepared by ten o'clock. At that hour Mrs. Bentley, our housekeeper, would call old Tom, the coachman, and hand him a large wicker basket swathed with snowy damask. In spite of its covering the basket exhaled such a delicious aroma that poor Tom was all but overcome by the time the carriage arrived at the mission. We then watched to see that Father Dunne ate his dinner instead of giving it away to some poor immigrant who had told him his troubles before or after Mass.

When the pastor of St. Columbkille's died, Father Dunne resigned his curacy in order to devote all his time to the swiftly increasing demands of the mission. Father Dunne was a blessing for the Italian Ameri-cans. He was a born linguist. During his student days in Rome he had acquired a fluent command of Italian. He could speak it in the accents of the Roman and

Rev. Edmund M. Dunne, D.D., about 1903.

north Italian haut ton, the dialects of the Neapolitans, Calabrians, and Sicilians; and he quickly lined up errant members of his new parish by lecturing them in the expressive Italian-American argot of Forquer Street.

Father Dunne was of medium height with strong and regular features. His shoulders were wide enough for the new burdens he had taken on. He had a very determined chin and deep-set eyes which were illumined in their depths by good humor and the light of benevolence. He had dark brown hair and eyes not too different from the Latins. He had secured a Doctor of Divinity degree from the American College in Rome. He also had a deep humility which hid his learning from his generally illiterate flock. Father Dunne was a natural pastor to his new flock. Not only did he know his parishioners by their first names, he also knew most of the influential businessmen and politicians of the city. One can see

that Archbishop Feehan did my mother and her aides
a good turn by suggesting Father Dunne as their mission's spiritual director. He could buttonhole any influential person he needed to in order to get Francisco a
job, get Tomaso out of a citizenship difficulty, or ease
an immigrant family past the importunities of the
padrone. And like a true priest he never overlooked
the essential. He had everyone in our Italian-American neighborhood building toward the future when
they would have their own church and parish school
and have every member of the family at Mass on
Sundays and holy days.

When Father Dunne came to us he was the sole
shepherd of Holy Guardian Angel Mission. As time
went on and the congregation increased, he still carried on alone except for aid on Sunday Masses. These
soon came to four of a Sunday, and Father Dunne
preached the sermon at each one. Three of these
sermons would be in Italian. The sermon at the
children's Mass was in English. Father Dunne realized it was more comforting to the older parishioners
to hear the word of God in their native tongue, but he
wished the children to become familiar with the
speech of their own new country. Father Dunne's
sermons, mother was never tired of repeating, were
extremely simple and direct. So were the little homi-
lies he was wont to give to the classes preparing for
their first holy communion. He had the art of instantly touching the heartstrings of the Italian-American children. His favorite topic was the Good Shepherd. From his own manly heart he drew for the
children the lessons of Jesus' love for little ones.
It was, he told them, greater than the love of a child
for a mother, or mother for a child; and because it
was so, the love of Jesus would reach out and follow
them their whole life long into eternity.

Mother and her assistants had feared failure; but
thanks to Father Dunne and his efforts, the congregation kept expanding. After a few months the little
chapel on the second floor of Holy Guardian Angel
School was too small, and all concerned saw that a

parish church was absolutely necessary. Father Dunne's parish was now the second largest Italian-American parish in the city.

Archbishop Feehan gave permission to Father Dunne and his coworkers to erect a parish church but he could not extend much financial assistance. Father Dunne therefore buttonholed influential friends right and left as did mother and her aides of the Children of Mary. All the alumnae of the Academy of the Sacred Heart were canvassed persistently. Pews were promised, a pipe organ donated. Finally, friends of Holy Guardian Angel Mission combined their resources and arranged a large loan for Father Dunne. A lot was purchased and plans ordered for a church with a five-hundred-person seating capacity and parish rectory.

Holy Guardian Angel Church stood on Forquer Street a few doors west of Desplaines Street, its main facade to the north. In architecture it was and is severely plain. The architect ambitiously termed his design "Lombardian Romanesque," which was subtle flattery. Actually, while Father Dunne strove for a facade and campanile that would be reminiscent of Italy, I must confess that much of the Holy Guardian Angel Church was and is a hybrid of architecture which one might term "American Economic." It was built of brick with very little stone trimming. It was simple in every way and mother was glad it was so. What decoration it needed was supplied by statues of Christ, his mother, and his foster father. The Bambino was there, symbol of the eternal Bethlehem. The altars with their paper flowers would have shocked liturgical aesthetics. But the parishioners of Holy Guardian Angel were too poor to purchase real flowers out of season, and the paper flowers were made by the loving hands of Italian mothers and their daughters. The brass candlesticks were polished to a luster by the ladies of the Altar Society.

Father Dunne always erred on the off side of prudence where anything like personal comfort and ambition were concerned. At first he thought he had

Holy Guardian Angel Church, 717 Forquer Street, Chicago.

Interior of Holy Guardian Angel Church.

been too ambitious with respect to the erection of the church, that he had constructed it on too broad a plan. Yet in five years after its consecration the church facilities had become taxed to the utmost. From an original estimate of four hundred parishioners, 350 of congregation and forty Sunday school pupils, there were one thousand families registered in Holy Guardian Angel parish in 1903 and 1415 children attending our Sunday school.

By 1903 Father Dunne's church was filled and emptied five times of a Sunday morning. In summer there would be about five weddings a week, in winter five funerals. Every Sunday afternoon two hours were set aside for christenings. On Sunday evenings there would be Vespers, the congregational singing of the Psalms, and Benediction of the Blessed Sacrament. All week long there were parish societies to supervise, consultations with mother and her mission aides, catechists to be assigned, catechism to be taught to old and young, visits to the sick and infirm, work to be found for fathers of families, education for immigrants black sheep had to be eased past courts and jails, the imprisoned visited, the parish accounts balanced, and more aid sought from wealthy Chicagoans. And there were a thousand and one other things Father Dunne had to do.

Mother told me that in 1903, five years after Holy Guardian Angel Church was founded, she had 115 assistants for her work at the mission. Under Father Dunne's direction these helpers taught catechism and bible history to children and adults at the Sunday school. Classes followed the nine o'clock Mass on Sundays and were also conducted weekday evenings for working people.

The volunteer assistants came from all parts of the city, from all walks of life, from among the clergy and religious and lay people. Some walked five miles to teach their catechism students on Sunday. That was the era of the cable car and carriages, but many of mother's aides had no access to cable cars and not all the alumnae of the Academy of the

Father Dunne and altar boys at Holy Guardian Angel Church.

Sacred Heart could afford carriages. But even for those who could, it was a two-hour ride to Forquer Street from the North Side, and an entire morning was lost riding in from Lake Forest. Some of these volunteers not only prepared their charges for holy communion, they also furnished the dress or the suit for that blessed event in the child's life.

In another way the influx of such assistants from all walks of life, non-Catholic as well as Catholic, and many from the higher strata of the city's social and business life was a blessing for the mission. Mother often said that these people helped Father Dunne impress upon our Italian Americans that Roman Catholics were as American as any of the social workers in the Protestant or secular social settlements hard by the mission.

I should like to pause here and mention the name of Elizabeth Smyth and the countless catechists who assisted mother and Father Dunne to instruct our people at Holy Guardian Angel's. They gave of self and time without stint. But they now have their names writ large by the recording angel in God's book of life and I can only breathe the age-old prayer of our Church for them: May eternal light shine upon them, O Lord. May they rest in peace.

Giuseppe and Lena Letizia from the province of Salerno who lived on DeKoven Street and whose first child, Charles, was baptized by Father Dunne in the Principal's Office of Guardian Angel School, 1897.

How To Pay the Bills?
The Charity Ball and Italian Bazaar 5

The church, school, and rectory of the Holy Guardian Angel now made an imposing group. Since over twenty thousand dollars had been spent on the site, the church, the rectory, and refurnishing of part of the school for our use, one might ask, how did Father Dunne and my mother pay the bills? Could they ever look forward to a time when Holy Guardian Angel parish would not be in hot water?

For a time mother wondered. She prayed hard every night to Our Lady of Perpetual Help before the white marble statue in her little oratory at home, hoping that by storming heaven with prayer she could secure the much needed financial assistance which was hindering the parish's further development. Since God helps those who help themselves, mother as well as father realized that a continuous, vigorous effort would have to be made to meet the interest payments and ordinary expenses of the mission. Father Dunne turned every stipend into the cashbox and he resolutely worked for nothing. His cassocks shaded from black to green until they wore out. If it were not for mother and Mrs. Bentley, he might have starved.

It finally dawned on mother and father that since they had assumed the duty of the mission, the burden of helping to maintain it was to be their cross. The results could not be measured by dollars in the treasury. A direct mail appeal was made on March 18, 1901 which netted the mission $481.50. Yet in 1901 there were about 750 children at the nine o'clock Masses on Sundays. By 1901 250 children had been prepared for their first holy communion and there were many belated first communions among the adult

First Communion Sunday, Guardian Angel Church, 1903.

parishioners. On his pastoral visit in 1900 Archbishop
Feehan had confirmed 491 people, of that number 61
were adults. This was the only sort of achievement
that could have satisfied Father Dunne, mother and
father, and all the catechists at Holy Guardian Angel's.
The humble mission with its vast potential for good
had become a challenge to social-minded Christians,
many not of our own faith.

Time after time I would hear mother say to father:
"There are so many bills to meet. Are you sure there
is no idle money in the bank account?" (With mild
reproach) "No, my dear Agnes, not a dollar. I gave
you a large check last month, remember? What is
left now is the absolute minimum necessary to carry
on the household." Mother would pucker her brow.
"Of course, I'd forgotten. But I wonder if the Blessed
Virgin knows how low we are in funds."

It was a comfort to watch mother at prayer. Somehow I felt that as bad as things might be neither she

nor father nor any of the good workers at the mission
would be called upon to bear more than they could.
But as if to try their faith, the cashbox would become
all but empty and the need for money become truly
desperate. At such times mother would enlist the
aid of Our Lady of Perpetual Help and then walk
around the room eyeing the pictures of Christ and
this or that saint, or she would take the holy pictures
of yet other saints out of her prayer book to beg their
intercession.

Mother's prayers were usually answered in spirit
and in material matters as well. Thus on one most
depressing Monday morning this letter came to mother
from the apostolic delegate:

Washington, D.C.

My dear Madame,

I have received your letter of March 17th with enclosed circular. I am glad to learn of the zealous
and fruitful work which is being done under the
guidance and encouragement of your Reverend
Pastor, Fr. Dunne, for the poor Italians of the
West Side of Chicago. I enclose a small offering,
and only wish that I could make it larger. With it
goes my earnest blessing and my best wish for
the further success of your work.

Most faithfully yours in Christ,
Sebastian Martinelli, D.D.

Then there was encouragement for mother in the
telegram she received from her friend Father Dumbach
one day in 1906 announcing that a mission for Italian
Americans was being founded in Pasadena following
the pattern of Holy Guardian Angel's. It opened with
forty-eight children in attendance and classes for first
communicants were starting immediately.

There was also the Christmas when the mission
funds were very low and many of our tots were un-

remembered. In the midst of the depression over not being able to remember more of the little charges with gift packages, along came the girls from St. Scholastica's Academy laden down with a vast supply of popcorn and Cracker Jack, ties, handkerchiefs, greeting cards, and other delightful miscellany for five hundred little ones.

Such manna from heaven encouraged mother to recruit new friends and acquaintances for work at the mission; or in lieu of that, they were asked to give financial support.

There were other sources of funds which assisted the mission. At the turn of the century a wave of distinguished high church Episcopalian converts entered the Roman Catholic Church. One of the most outstanding of these was Dr. Benjamin De Costa who had entered the fold in 1899. The mission sponsored his lecture on "America--Historic, Social, Religious" which proved a godsend for him as well as for the mission. Every seat at Powers Theater that Sunday afternoon was sold and extra chairs all but crowded Dr. De Costa off the stage.

By November 1899 the mission indebtedness had been reduced to $9,000 and the major portion of the debt on the church was paid off. The church was consecrated on November 28, 1899 by Archbishop Feehan. This was very encouraging to Father Dunne as well as to father and mother. But having accomplished so much my dear mother felt no desire to rest but was only recharged for the additional work she had yet to do. That is why I find among my mementoes of 1899 an engraved invitation begging the recipient and his lady to favor the patronesses of Holy Guardian Angel Mission with the honor of their attendance at the Charity Dance to be held in the Banquet Hall of the Auditorium Hotel. This was succeeded the following year by a Charity Ball held in the same hotel. This socially successful event scarcely made enough money to pay our fuel bills for that winter. What to do? Few of our parishioners at the mission could pay pew rent. A collection at the children's Mass was resolutely avoided. Yet the need for funds remained.

Mother hesitated to inaugurate any immediate successors to the Charity Ball because of unjust criticism which had arisen, the worst attack the infant mission had to withstand. Although most of the Catholics in Chicago were in favor of the mission and its purposes, some detractors within our fold together with some enemies outside strove to oppose our entire procedure on the grounds of inutility and segregation! We were ridiculed as socialite settlement workers, exploiters of the poor Italian Americans we sought to serve, and charged with trying to isolate them from their fellow American citizens. We were taunted with the failure of our efforts, since as the detractors pointed out, Italian Americans were still trash, "Wops," and "Dagos," no matter what one did with them.

All these facts were behind the opening of the bazaar to aid the Italian mission which was held in the home of my parents, 449 North State Street [later numbered 1301] on the afternoon and evening of November 17, 1904. It was, in the words of the society editor of the Inter-Ocean, "one of the largest home bazaars of the season." The doors were opened to guests at one o'clock and from then until eleven our friends crowded the house. While invitations had been issued, the bazaar was deliberately made most informal. Mother and father and their coworkers had built up the mailing list to invite every friend and benefactor they could think of. The Italian supper, which was to be served from six to eight o'clock, included all sorts of Italian foods from antipastos to genuine spumoni.

For the bazaar mother and father had converted the entire English basement of our home into an autumn bower with brilliantly colored oak leaves that had been gathered in the country the day before. There were booths on the first floor of the house for various kinds of gifts to be sold during the bazaar. Each booth was a veritable oak-leaf bower in itself. Mrs. John P. Byrne had charge of the booth displaying infants' wear. Katherine Wade was in charge of the doll palace with Margaret Tait, Elizabeth Rend, Robert C. Newton, and myself assisting. Sales at the neckwear and handkerchief booth were under the direction of Mabel Hannah, assisted by Lillian Inderrieden, Mrs. David Swing Ricker, and my sister Charlotte. The society editor of the Chicago Journal reported that, "Miss Hannah never had been formally introduced to the polite world"; but lack of such exposure never troubled our dear Hannah Webb. She was a born saleswoman.

Mrs. Edward Osgood Brown in her native Italian costume had complete charge of the dining room in the oak-leaf garlanded basement. Also in Italian garb were her assistants Adelaide Walsh, May O'Meara, Constance Walsh, Ellen Corse, and Cora Prindiville. Extraordinary arrangements had been made to serve our guests properly. In spite of the fact some of our newspaper friends waggishly wrote that "nonunion waitresses were employed at Amberg's Italian Restaurant," certain politicians with powerful labor connections ate heartily of our Italian viands, all expertly prepared by Italian chefs. The entire affair was a great success, socially and personally. But to be practical I should perhaps record that it netted the mission only $257.00 over and above expenses.

I thought of the matrons and misses who had given long weeks of preparation, the helpers who had taken time off from work to bring oak leaves in from the country. I thought of the handmade dolls attired in clothes lacy with exquisite needlework, the best specimens of which remained unsold. However, when the bazaar was over mother and her aides sent everything that was left over to St. Vincent's Orphan Asylum for its own bazaar which was to be held in December. The charming dolls and other exquisite handicraft thus found a possibly wider field of purchasers.

The financial nest egg from the bazaar should have remained intact. But the mission activities expanded so rapidly that in a short time the finances of the mission were exactly where they had been before.

As father insisted, something like a regularly sustained financial effort would have to be made if the mission were to continue. Mother and her assistants decided that the bazaar, which brought much welcome newspaper publicity for the mission, had demanded work far out of proportion to the proceeds on hand. The charity ball, the bazaar, and other fund-raising social activities eventually developed into the annual tea dance given by the Madonna Auxiliary.

Amberg family with Bishop Dunne at Mackinac Island home, 1908. Standing: Genevieve Amberg Cremin, Mrs. William A. Amberg, Bishop Dunne, John Ward Amberg. Seated: William A. Amberg, Mary Agnes Amberg, Mrs. John W. Amberg. Children: Bertrand, Agnes, and Mary Barbara Amberg.

I suppose it was natural that around the turn of the century Chicago should hold within its borders the largest Sunday school in the world. Twelve years had passed since mother and her helpers had entered the Italian-American community on the West Side and gathered in the first of forty little ones for catechism class in Guardian Angel Mission on Forquer Street. Now in 1910 there was a church, a parish hall, and a rectory; and the continuing influx of Italian Americans kept the congregation growing. Seventeen hundred and more children now attended the Sunday school and they mushroomed everywhere: into the library, the halls, Father Dunne's office, even into the boiler room. What mother and her aides had accomplished at Guardian Angel Mission was indeed notable, even outside church circles. The Chicago Tribune of March 20, 1910 ran a large feature article on the Sunday school.

Before I go on with this chronicle I should perhaps explain that our neighborhood was not the only large Italian-American community in Chicago at the time, and mother and her aides were not the sole pioneers of settlement work among the Italian Americans in Chicago. Our dear friend Rebecca Gallery had been serving the Italian Americans in the neighborhood around Casa Maria for years. The workers at Guardian Angel Mission were glad to share in a common effort to educate a fine immigrant people in its ancient faith. It is hard to ascertain definitely just when the mission grew beyond a Sunday school and became a social settlement. I shall try to draw the picture as best I can. But first I want to pick up some considerations I touched upon earlier.

The lot of the immigrant is a lonely one. The Italian immigrant laborer was at the mercy of the padrone system. Americans often assume their way of life is superior to all others, and that the immigrant, the newcomer, is a misfit.

Because of this immigrant families and their neighbors cling with a fierce tenacity to their old ways in the new land. Thus in "Little Italy" the people cluster around their padrones in solid groups of Neapolitans, Calabrians, and Sicilians, and are slow to learn the American way of life. Some of the older people never learned English. Schools had kindergartens for the younger children and language classes for the older ones. But evening classes for adults were overlooked.

Mother had always been aware of this defect in the Americanization process. What brought it to a sharp focus was a twenty-year-old Italian American who came to the mission one day and begged her to teach him to write his name in English and help him learn a few short business phrases in English. With these he could get a job as a teamster with a commission firm dealing in fruits and vegetables on South Water Street. This fragrant street lies along the south side of the river just north of the Loop. This was for a long time Chicago's principal fruit and vegetable market. Mother realized that the farm-bred Italian Americans, with a little help, could do well in the market.

Mother decided that a night school was absolutely necessary for the adult immigrants. The young teamster was to be the advance guard of a small army of Italian Americans whom mother and her aides would assist in learning the language of their new country. Since the mission's resources were already taxed to the limit, mother cast about for likely night school accommodations. Almost directly across the street from Holy Guardian Angel Church stood the Dante Public School, serving the children of the neighborhood during the day, but idle in the evening. Charles A. Plamondon, father of my friend Marie Plamondon, was vice president of the Board of Education at the time. In 1903 mother applied through him to use one of the rooms for night classes in English. She hoped that the Board would supply the textbooks as she was prepared to furnish the teachers. But E. G. Dooley, then superintendent of schools, had to refuse since there were no funds available at the time. Mr. Plamondon's representations were of no avail.

But William J. Bogan, then principal of the Washington Elementary School, assisted mother and her aides to secure teachers and books and everything else necessary to teach English reading and writing and elementary civil government. They soon had the night school for adults a going concern in the basement of Guardian Angel Church. One hundred students registered for the first classes and the number increased thereafter.

A year after its first refusal, the Board of Education had practical evidence of the value of our adult classes. The mission had to carry on as best it could with the adult educational program. The Board later opened the Dante School to mother and Mr. Bogan and their aides for a summer vacation school for children.

If mother had not gained all she had hoped for, the vacation school was something, and it made her very happy. Mr. William J. Bogan placed everything he could at our disposal. About 650 children registered on our opening day early in July 1904. Since we made no religious or racial distinction, all faiths and races were represented. We had Irish, Polish, German, Jewish, and Bohemian children as well as Italian Americans. Miss Gilmore, the principal of the vacation school, immediately started a home economics course by converting three of the classrooms into a sitting-dining room, a bedroom, and a kitchen. The girls made curtains for the windows, hemmed table and bed linen, made dresses for themselves, together with handbags, vanity cases, sachets, and the like. By the end of the summer little girls had been taught washing, ironing, bedmaking, scrubbing, light cooking, dressmaking, millinery, and so on. They also received a short course in infant care and personal hygiene. As for the boys, our principal effort was to keep their active bodies occupied with useful play. We had swift reviews of schoolwork, taught manual arts and handicraft. We arranged picnics and ball games and hikes to the park and the lakefront. Everyone accomplished something. At the end of the vacation school handsomely printed certificates were distributed to each pupil and honorable awards were given to those with a perfect attendance record. Mr. Bogan and Mortimer C. Watters graded the children, helped Miss Gilmore make assignments, and above all insisted that the teachers give just marks.

In the vacation schools of the mission the public school teachers of our faith, of differing faiths, of no faith shared the teacher's platform with nuns, Jesuit scholastics, and Christian Brothers. The common ambition of all was the Americanization of their pupils. Miss Gilmore reported that "Our little folks are most happy in their summer course. The teachers say they never worked with more appreciative pupils."

But we were always plagued by limited funds. Other nearby settlements were more grandly organized, generously subsidized, and had more to offer than mother could give her charges. On Sundays, for instance, she added a storytelling hour to counteract the pull of a certain denominational social settlement in the neighborhood. All the other social settlements not only had vacation schools, but days in the country, parties and picnics, and plentiful recreational resources available through the donations of public-spirited citizens. Whereas the Guardian Angel Mission had all it could do to survive financially. Our teachers expanded their activities at the mission to counteract the attraction of other neighborhood centers. But mother's hope was with the children. It was a daily source of wonder for mother and her helpers to see how such responsive, affectionate, bright, and docile children could develop under the sordid conditions of Forquer Street. They were worth striving and working for.

In 1905 mother would be precipitated into a chaotic world of farewells and leave-takings and uprootings and loneliness. In her case the blow was double-edged. She was informed by the Chancery Office that the Guardian Angel school building on Forquer Street would have to be abandoned and that Father Dunne was to become chancellor of the archdiocese.

Our people were crushed, the old parishioners as well as the children. How could they ever exist without this grand priest who was their doctor of divinity, of Americanization, of everything else? Could anyone ever again be like Father Dunne? Could anyone short of an archangel be as swift as Father Dunne in scaling down the financial exactions of the padrone, in forcing elementary rights from the alderman, in securing a good lawyer, in posting one's bond? No, there would never be another like Father Dunne.

After Father Dunne left us, Father Pacifico Chenuil, C.S.C.B., came to take his place as spiritual director of the mission and to serve Holy Guardian Angel parish. Archbishop Feehan had died on January 8, 1903 and was succeeded by the Most Reverend James Quigley, the former bishop of Buffalo. It was while he was in Buffalo that Archbishop Quigley became acquainted with Father Chenuil's work among the Italian Americans there.

Our people missed Father Dunne very much, but were all very glad to have a pastor of their own race. Father Chenuil was a good priest and an excellent administrator. During his pastorate the basement of Holy Guardian Angel Church was excavated and a chapel constructed for the children's Mass. The chapel also became a meeting hall for the parish. Father Chenuil made other improvements in the

the church and rectory and paid off a great portion
of the debt.

Our Italian Americans were very pleased with
Father Chenuil, but he would have been at a great
disadvantage without the loyal helpers and teachers
of the Sunday school. Mother and I had loving mem-
ory of Mary Mannering and her assistants, Julia
Garvy, Eleanor Doyle, Rose Murphy, Francis
Colemen, Clio Manner, Ella Conway, Charles Doyle,
Edward Delbacaro, and William J. Bogan. Thomas
Shea had charge of the evening classes for the boys
and girls and the adult pupils.

Finally, as if to make providential amends to
them for taking Father Dunne away, mother related
that the first Christmas of Father Chenuil's pastorate
[1905] found them all more at ease in mind and pocket than they had been for many a day. There was a
beautiful Christmas tree, 2,230 children received
holy communion, and each received a box of candy
and a useful gift. The twelve altar boys each received a new suit of clothes.

While mother and her aides had not been happy
about the loss of Guardian Angel school building,
they were entirely satisfied with the mission's
priestly helpers. In addition to Father Chenuil,
Father H. J. Dumbach, S.J., of St. Ignatius College
showed a lively interest in our undertaking. As a
result by 1907 one of the Jesuits was coming regularly
on Sunday mornings to speak to our children at Mass.
And five afternoons each week for the two months
prior to first holy communion, Jesuit priests and
scholastics came to give the new communicants
religious instruction. The Jesuit Fathers also gave
a mission this year at Holy Guardian Angel for the
children. The church was crowded to capacity. In
1907 we began to secure the help of the Christian
Brothers and the Sisters of Charity of the Blessed
Virgin Mary as well as substantial numbers of their
students.

Around 1910-1911 mother had toyed with the idea
of a permanent resident to direct the mission's ever-

widening activities. And about that time word came
to mother from the archdiocese that quarters for a
mission resident were available for a small rental
in St. Francis of Assisi School on Newberry Street
just south of Twelfth Street. The school had been
closed since the influx of Polish and Russian Jews
in the neighborhood.

While I was in the city between a sojourn in
Pennsylvania and a trip to Florida, I rode over with
mother and Catherine Jordan to see the school. We
had passed the place before, but had given it no
thought whatsoever because of its desolation,
dinginess, and desertion. This day in late November
it was more depressing than ever. The windowpanes
were dirty, the doors creaked, the rats scurried
away when we came in.

The classrooms were large and well proportioned
however. This had once been a German parish planned
on a vast and practical scale. There were eight classrooms, each thirty feet square, and in its day every
one of the thirty-two desks in each of the eight rooms
had been filled with pupils. But the school, while no
longer used for its primary purpose, was not altogether deserted. A Saenger-Verein still used one
of the rooms and other German-American organizations used the premises now and then.

Some months later I became a resident of an
"apartment" in the school with Catherine Jordan to
facilitate our services at the mission. Mr. Bogan,
then principal of Lane Technical High School, was
appalled that I and my fellow resident should slumber
alone and unprotected in the deserted school in that
rather tough area of the city. To foil the rodents
in the building Mr. Bogan bought and supplied
numerous rattraps. And to keep out human intruders,
he concocted a most ingenious burglar alarm, calculated to go off if anybody entered the outside door
of the four-room apartment Catherine and I had
constructed in one of the classrooms. This was all
very reassuring but there was no need for it, as
no one ever molested Catherine Jordan or myself.

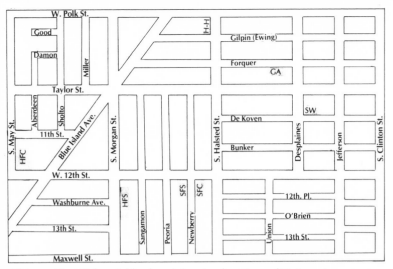

Chicago West Side neighborhood showing locations of St. Francis School, Guardian Angel Church, and Holy Family Church.

St. Francis of Assisi School, 1226 South Newberry Street, opened in 1881.

But one night the provost of the Saenger-Verein let himself into the school earlier than his comrades in order to build a fire, and by mistake he opened the door of our apartment in the dark. Suddenly the cavernous old building resounded with the most alarming clatter I have ever heard, and the last we saw of the provost was his dark shadow speeding down the hallway, down the stairs, passing the lamplight below, and on down the street. I am sorry Mr. Bogan never took out a patent on his burglar alarm; it would have made him rich.

Early in 1912 we began the Guardian Angel's Social Center in two classrooms in the St. Francis of Assisi school building at 1226 South Newberry Street. The social center was an extension of the work of the mission on Forquer Street.

The original two rooms were quickly extended to five and were used for reading, billiards, sewing classes, and club meetings. One room was used as the living quarters for the resident directors of the mission, Catherine Jordan and myself. But more about that in the next chapter. Once a week the large auditorium on the third floor was rented for dancing or an entertainment.

The social center featured sewing, dancing, and raffia classes for girls in the afternoons, debating and social clubs for older boys and girls in the evenings, and dressmaking classes for young working women.

The center was imperative if the boys and girls were to be saved from all that was unwholesome in their environment and if the efforts of the five proselytizing missions in the neighborhood were to be counteracted. Some had clubs, sewing classes, and so on.

The work of Guardian Angel's Mission and Social Center continued spiritually through the Sunday school, intellectually through the library, and socially through its many clubs and classes until 1917. In that year the influx of Italians into the Newberry Street neighborhood demanded that all the rooms in St. Francis School be used for the parish school, and the Guardian Angel Social Center had to move to other quarters. But I am now getting ahead of my story and must go back a little.

My Decision To Become Permanent Resident, 1913

Holy Guardian Angel's was begun as a mission to instruct Italian Americans in their faith, but in the course of a decade or so it developed many of the activities proper to a social settlement except that it claimed no permanent residents on the premises. As I muse over those hectic days, I do not believe mother fully realized all the facets of neighborhood usefulness her initial catechetical project had acquired. It was natural for her to view the mission's developments in quite another light, in many ways the mission approximated the character of a religious foundation. The workers were all volunteers activated by a spiritual impulse much as if they were religious men and women. No one had taken any special vows, they wore no habit, some of the volunteers in fact were not Roman Catholic, and yet they looked upon their work with the children and adults of the neighborhood as a vocation. Each day's work began, so far as it was practicable, with attendance at Mass and the reception of holy communion.

As usual, it was mother who first sensed, if not the mission's trend, at least its evident limitations. Her mission project had expanded miraculously in spite of all sorts of hazards. Its very size was terrific; and it required so much time and attention. I knew from her worried look that mother had become afraid of her helpers' abilities to nurse along the Gargantuan infant of their own creation. I had been able to sense this strain in mother perhaps sooner than she herself, or father, or our friends did. For most of my adult years I had been com-

muting from our North State Street home to this or
that city, to the home of this or that relative, this
or that resort, in what I can now appraise as a very
selfish young woman's search for health. Foolish
and self-willed as my actions were, my self-
indulgence did not blind me utterly. From the
perspective which my long absences lent to my view
of her, I could detect certain alarming changes in
mother. There never had been for me quite such
another marvel as she. Like Jane Addams she
wasted no time 'twixt rising and breakfasting, could
complete her toilette for the day and be off about her
business while the ordinary sort of woman would be
studying the merits of two different shades of mas-
cara. With the perspective I gained from my absences, I could see the crow's-feet creeping more
closely around her eyes, she easily became irritated,
there were more streaks of silver in her hair. But
this was all the perspective my love for her gave
me at the time. I was well on my way to becoming
that silliest of creatures, a society bird of passage,
without strong home ties and ever eager to seek
a new roost among distant friends and acquaintances
far from Chicago.

When mother finally realized that the mission had
grown to such proportions as to make a permanent
directress and staff of resident workers advisable,
she acted with her usual directness. If the Forquer
Street quarters offered no room for them, why not
try another way? Some years before a community of
women called the Little Helpers of the Holy Souls
had been formed in Paris. It was a Roman Catholic
religious order whose members wore the customary
nun's habit but whose activities were to a great ex-
tent extramural as compared with those of most
sisterhoods. Mother's very dear friends, Reverend
Mother Dupont of the Academy of the Sacred Heart,
Lake Forest, Miss Mary Merrick, president of the
Christ-Child Society in Washington, and Mrs. Charles
Cavanagh of our city gave mother such glowing accounts of the Helpers that mother decided to invite

them to Holy Guardian Angel Mission as a logical extension of their order's work in America.

For certain reasons, all good and excellent, the superior of the Helpers found herself unable to accept mother's proposal. I happened to be at home in Chicago between some of my interminable commutings when mother received the foreign-looking envelope with the Paris postmark. After mother read the letter and laid it aside, I read it myself. All that day mother remained downcast, though none of her charges at the mission would have guessed it from her cheerful conversation and disposition. When I went in to kiss her good night at the end of the day, I found she had been praying longer than usual before the image of Our Lady of Perpetual Help. Father was still sitting up in the library going over a portfolio of work he had brought home from the office, and we discussed the depressing effect upon mother of the letter she had received that day. Father did not agree that the superior's letter held any note of finality; he felt that mother should not have taken things so much to heart. He considered mother's consecration to her mission was fully as potent before God as the work of the Little Helpers or any other religious community. This was our conclusion. We both hastened to mother with it, anxious to ease her mind and ensure her rest for the night. We found her bright and thankful; but, I thought, quite unconvinced. It was as though somewhere along the line she felt she had failed.

Mother felt indisposed the next morning, but after attending to her household affairs and planning the day for the servants, she rode to the mission. Contrary to her custom, however, she had Old Tom our coachman call for her early in the afternoon. As she did not look at all well, I saw her into the carriage and remained at the mission in her stead. Our friend, Mr. Bogan, who had come to discuss vacation school plans with mother, reassured her anxiety and promised to drive me home later. Mr. Bogan managed to put mother into her usual happy frame of mind before she left, but as we watched Old Tom and our team of bays bear her away, the face of the man beside me was suddenly grave and concerned.

"I suppose, Mary, you know that your mother is one in a million," remarked Mr. Bogan.

"I know it," I said.

"It's strange, Mary, isn't it, that you can see the same person every day and then one day you see them with new eyes?" He took my hand. "Mary, my dear girl, today for the first time I realized that your mother has grown old amongst us. Her spirit will never grow old. But she has carried the vast affairs of the mission almost single-handedly these past fifteen years, and the task has taken its toll of her. Have you thought, Mary," he continued, "what would happen to the mission if God ever calls your mother away?"

"It will go on," I proffered stubbornly. "It always has."

"Yes, my dear, but not in the way it could go." He released my hand abruptly sensing that I had drawn away. "Where do you expect to go? What are your plans for the summer, Mary?"

"I really can't say," I told him petulantly. "I am due at Mount Pleasant Villa with Marie Plamondon for a two-week visit. Afterward, if it is not too hot, I was going to visit Uncle Bill in Texas."

"For your health, I presume?"

"Of course," I rejoined.

"And be happy?" he bantered.

"Naturally."

"I'll tell you something about happiness, Mary," said Mr. Bogan. "Since I began helping your mother with the Sunday school, I have never been happier in my life. The essence of happiness is service to others. I haven't neglected my work at the high school, Mary. But I would not neglect my work here. I try to tell myself I am sacrificing my night's sleep by working here, that a man of my age needs eight hours of sleep if he is to work the next day. But I

happen to know that your mother has gotten along
with four, or five, or six hours of sleep every
day for years. Anyone in this neighborhood can tell
you by looking out their windows at night; it isn't
a milkman or a gangster going by, it's your mother
and Mrs. Bentley and Old Tom on this or that errand
of mercy. As if the day's work at the mission was
not enough for her."

"I know," I agreed. "Mother cannot spare herself
in the face of another's need or trouble."

"You are like your mother, Mary," resumed Mr.
Bogan, "not in her drive and sense of direction,
perhaps; but that isn't needed anymore. Your mother
established the mission's momentum. And you and I
and the other helpers have been geared to it. Besides
our people know you and love you and are used to
you." He reached for my hand again, as if to prevent
my raising it to ward off his next blow. "Tell me,
Mary, something we all want to know. The mission
needs a permanent resident to focus its expanding
activities. Your mother has done more than her
share. But she has coached you well, and you fit in
so well with the needs of our people. Tell me, Mary,
why don't you quit that butterfly chasing for health
and come here as a permanent resident of the mission? At least for a while."

"Is that why you sent mother on ahead?" I asked
him. It was a warm August night; there was not a
breeze stirring. I dabbed the perspiration from my
brow. The nerve of him. Was it not just like a man
urging a residency at the mission for me, Mary
Amberg, when anyone could see there was no room.
Was he imagining that I could live at the back of the
church? My words stormed and tumbled as I told
him so.

"Perhaps yes, Mary," he agreed, but not con-
tritely. "What was it Napoleon said? 'Circumstances?
I make circumstances.'" He smiled boyishly. "I'm
no Napoleon, Mary, but I do admire your mother.
And of all the persons I know, I believe that you are
the one most qualified to carry on at the mission."

William J. Bogan

He took his handkerchief and patted his brow. "Well,
it's done. Let's stop at Tony's for an ice cream
soda and I'll drive you home."

It was not a pleasant drive, even along North State
Street where I felt the cool breeze from the lake.
All the way from the mission and as I tossed in bed
that night, I was rebellious and resentful. I imputed
motives to the fine man I respected like a father.
I could not believe Mr. Bogan's suggestion had been
casual. It must have been some well-laid plan of
the mission workers to destroy my chance for good

health and my peace of mind. I was not wise enough
to know that dear Mr. Bogan had that night snatched
a very self-indulgent young miss from the chance to
become a self-centered old hypochondriac sitting on
resort hotel porches telling everyone about her
latest operation. I felt that I had been put up in a
tree, without realizing that it was from such a van-
tage point that a certain Zacchaeus saw his Lord.

Christ came into the picture Mr. Bogan had
painted for me, and I could not drive him away.
The symbol brought with it all sorts of troubling
images. Hitherto I had not actually disliked the work
at the mission so long as I could take it on when I
wished and leave it when I desired. On that basis
the responsibilities were not mine. But in the wake
of this troubling conversation I saw myself crucified
to the ever-present demands of the mission. I had
not thought of this aspect of mother's work before.
If I had cringed and run away from the continuing
grind, I had always felt that mother would remain
because she was stronger than I. But now I entered
a dark turmoil of spirit compounded of love for my
mother and an almost morbid preoccupation with
the conditions of our people's lives. I went to the
public library and got hold of some social literature,
read what the humanitarians were writing on the
subject of socioeconomic relations. The secular
humanists were all too puny, so I turned to Pope
Leo, read Rerum Novarum, read the interpretations
of our hierarchy, and strove to orient both the mission and myself in the broad Catholic scheme of life
which Mr. Bogan had hinted at.

But it did not seem to be of much use. I tried to
tell myself I did not need all that immersion in
social literature as I was a person of intense social
consciousness--even if I were a social butterfly.
Furthermore, everything I had read about the social
humanitarians left me without much anchorage. In
those days the name "social settlement," coined at
Toynbee Hall in London, was very new. Toynbee
Hall had been founded in London by Reverend

Mary Agnes Amberg at Mackinac Island around 1908.

Samuel A. Barnett, rector of the Anglican Church of
St. Jude. Unlike many clerics who would have accepted
a safe and comfortable living reading the gospel and
the epistle in the best Shakespearean mode, the
Reverend Barnett had gone back to the divinity schools
of Oxford and Cambridge and had persuaded the
young men that the gospel of Christ demanded social
action. The result was Toynbee Hall, a social settlement under Anglican auspices. Toynbee Hall had
nurtured a sudden swarm of social settlements,
notably Hull-House in Chicago; and it rapidly formed

the nucleus about which a whole new school of social literature was building up. But though it had caused social settlements to spread hope in the slums of London, New York, and Chicago, the term aroused suspicion among those Catholics who hesitate like the Pharisees and Sadducees to believe that anything good can come out of Nazareth. They resolutely blinded themselves to any Christian good fostered under any other than Catholic auspices.

But Mr. Bogan like Father Dunne was a good Catholic. And for two such fine men to understand what mother had attempted and recommend it to me implied, I fear, more responsibility in me than I really possessed. Many of our best friends thought the mission too expensive as well as premature. And it was, as father and mother knew all too well. To dramatize myself in the role of a darling daughter hurrying from her social travels to serve the children of mother's mission was fine if one lived in a land of daydreams. But the reality was full of insistences as subtle as they were cruel. I began to sense that I was drawing away from what conscience told me was my simple duty.

It would be very fine at this stage of my narrative if I were able to introduce the element of struggle and conflict, to portray an image of myself a-wrestle with Christ, as Jacob with the angel. I might raise the dread vision of dark years ahead of myself as a sourpuss resident of a social settlement, an aging spinster bereft of husband, children, home, and all life's social solaces. I am sorry, but it was all much simpler for me. I loved Christ then as I love him now. I was willing to place myself in his presence and abide by the counsels of my confessor. But in the dark night of the soul the sufferer stands and suffers alone. One's God seems absent. All reduces to the simple and ugly equation of self. Gethsemani was Christ's dark night of the soul, even those he loved had chosen sleep, and he had to fight things out alone. It is well, perhaps, that the agony in the garden is one of the sorrowful

mysteries. But in its loneliness and hopelessness,
then hope, it deserves its own rosary.

The first frightening vision in my dark night of the
soul concerned the mission's purely material needs.
Mammon always cares for the happy and well-dressed
scions of success. But Christ's dictum: "The poor ye
have always with ye," remains as his reminder to
the unsocial wealthy. It is the Christian's ever-
present challenge to more and more social effort.
I knew full well the story of mission bills overdue.
I knew the shame and evasions of placating creditors,
of making a dollar stretch out for ten when there
was not a penny in the cashbox. I wondered if I
could equal mother in such emergencies. For her
to look into the empty cashbox was simply another
incentive to pray: "Give us this day our daily bread."

By and by my meditation convinced me that much
of the mission's financial troubles had been due to
divided energies. We tried to serve the Italian Americans and live their life while clinging to our own.
One cannot, of course, live another's life. But there
is great merit in the full acceptance of responsibility,
as it carries much of its own momentum of action
and fulfillment. I began to see the need of an organization of helpers and residents at the settlement,
a closely knit organization right on the premises.

Mother must have realized that I was under a
strain. But with her beautiful sense of consideration
for another's feelings she never showed her concern.
If anything, she held herself too aloof. And I did
wish for sympathy, the reassuring pat of her hand
to let me know that she understood. It is strange
and appalling, this loneliness which must come to
full growth and yet leave the beholder unwitting,
even blind, before the unfolding tragedy of a human
life. The child of the family next door catches the
dread polio, a fatal auto accident robs a family
of its husband and loving father. A son dies in action
"over there." We imagine we shall never be left
alone during a crucifixion in our lives. Yet the
crisis does come, for in the dark night of the soul

the crucifixion comes at least once for everyone.
And while words of sympathy may help, they cannot
change one single pang.

My depression was profound for days. For a while
I went to the mission with mother every day; I played
the organ, taught, and kept the records listlessly.
I was appalled how little effect the tragedies told by
unfortunates seeking help at the mission had upon
my stony self. Never did I recall such dull, uninspiring holy communions, such distracted attendance
at Mass. I actually began to hate my mother and
Mr. Bogan, if that were possible, for preparing the
trap for me. I began to grow querulous and rebel-
lious about essentials of the faith whose wholesome-
ness I had always taken as a matter of course. I fell
into the sin of pessimism. "What's the use?" What
were we trying to do at the mission anyway? Produce
an upstanding class of high-grade laity? Parish
schools had been in existence all over the United
States long before Holy Guardian Angel's Mission,
long enough for millions of pupils to grow up and
make their outstanding mark upon the national life.
But I could not name one single parish school product,
one graduate whose name was nationally known.

It was only when I forced my sense of fairness to
come into play against the darkness that beset me
that I realized it was only after a period of doubt
and indecision that Christ told his disciples they would
become fishers of men. The Christian has no right to
measure his status in the community in terms of
leadership. "The kingdom of heaven is like leaven
which a woman takes and hides in three measures
of meal until the whole is leavened" (Matthew 13:33).
We at the mission and our charges were a leaven,
as the parish schools were a leaven of the local,
state, and national communities. Take us away,
and a more sluggish inertia of citizenship and morale
would be the fate of the mass.

I had scarcely resolved this latest doubt than
another difficulty loomed out of the dark night of
anxiety. What was Mr. Bogan suggesting, what was

my conscience suggesting, except that by becoming
a resident at the mission I was only pulling certain
ecclesiastical chestnuts out of the fire. The Sicilians,
the Neapolitans, the Calabrians had not come to
Chicago of their own will. The groundwork for their
arrival had been laid long before by a hierarchy
considering its own aggrandizement. Certainly the
Sicilians and the Calabrians should have been diverted
to homesteads, should have contributed to the farm-
ing backbone of the great Middle West. Instead they
had been diverted into the slum areas of the city.
And why? Because the hierarchy needed parishioners
to finance the vast parish projects, the schools,
churches, rectories, asylums, hospitals, convents,
and monasteries that were the outward and visible
form of the Church. But then I must be fair and not
impute a motive where none existed. The early
bishops might have been pleased if Francisco and
Maria could have been settled on farms. But they
were not above the difficulties of their time. The
industrialist looked to the immigrants for a vast
cheap labor pool and channeled them into the city at
a rate the churchmen never dreamed of.

From this bogeyman I passed on to another, the
transfixion we feel in the presence of a great individual and the pathetic idolatry we give to a great
man or woman, as if they could yield us secrets of
greatness we ourselves do not possess. We also
extend the cult of bigness to human institutions.
During this time I felt the need of long walks, any-
where and everywhere. Two blocks from the mission
lofted before me the lighted windows of Hull-House.
Mother and I knew Jane Addams and her coresidents
and coworkers well. All of us had looked upon Hull-
House as a challenge, yet we never experienced
anything but kindness and thoughtfulness and cooperation from Jane Addams. But as I would stand
outside Hull-House in the night looking at Chicago's
greatest and most publicized social settlement,
perfect in every avenue of its technique, I would
rebel. Why did we have to inhabit, only two blocks

Hull-House, Halsted Street between Polk and Ewing Streets, around 1920.

from this superb foundation, a shabby and unimpressive building ill fitted for our purpose? And our purpose was more sacred than the purely humanistic one of Hull-House, Chicago Commons, and the other social settlements.

By and by I learned the answer to that one also. I had fallen into the cult of mere size. Even today [1940], when we are all presumably better educated and more sophisticated, Chicagoans are inordinately proud that in their midst is the largest building in the world [the Merchandise Mart]. That it is as ugly and uninspiring as a toad squatting beside a riverbank makes no difference. It will be a long time before we are educated to seek not the biggest, but the finest building in a city.

I eventually saw that there was enough magic within the eyes of our youngsters to offset the appeal of the costly and gleaming equipment of Hull-House. Through our rehabilitated structures we and our children looked down vistas of grandeur too magnificent to paint. And indeed some of the non-Catholic residents of the social settlements came to see our vision and became, like Ellen Gates Starr of Hull-House, converts to our faith.

No, the heavily endowed social settlement did not matter. The apparent handicap of money, publicity, and prestige did not matter. We at the mission not only worked with splendid human timber, there was something finer and deeper, each person's immortal soul. We also had the advantage of a continuity of faith and its supranational nuances which, try as they might, the secular social settlements could not fully possess. The alert young university students sensed this also. Students of the social sciences came to the mission classes again and again to find what it was that others did not have that made our social settlement tick so harmoniously.

But many of our own faith were critical also and thought our ideas were premature. They were. The Christian who malingers is lost. "But," proffered our fair-weather friends, "one need not go about all one's life begging daily bread for those who do not deserve it. One only has to look a bit below the surface of things to discover that if an Italian dis-covered America, the Guineas had proceeded to make a gangster's paradise out of it. Statistics proved that the majority of gangsters, plus the high-jacking gentry, were of Italian origin."

The critics also cited the speedier tempo of Italian-American religious observance. In the shrines of "Little Italy" the vigil lights were perhaps gaudier and larger than in the high-class city areas. The holy pictures were luridly colored lithographs with biological Sacred Hearts and sadistic purgatorial scenes. The church societies do not march in stately procession behind priest and acolytes but resemble young David dancing before the ark to the sound of firecrackers and brass bands.

No matter how I cast up a tentative point sheet of pros and cons affecting my future at the mission, the pros exceeded the cons. But I remained rebel-lious. And the tug-of-war within me would begin again and cause another delay in decision.

Yet when I stopped to think of it, Christ had promised no bed of roses to his followers. There

are difficulties in all that he encouraged the Christian
to do; otherwise achievement would be as unsubstantial
as a jellyfish. Also, I do not think any love or demand of Christ was failing within my soul. I had always felt and considered Christ as my very near
and dear friend. My dark night, if I may call it that,
got all its umbrage and stumblings from my own
self-conceit and pride. I was, I hoped, thinking myself out of it, but was still hesitant. I held off from
any final commitment for the time being. I had
gained confidence but still felt spiritually unworthy.

One night before Christmas of that year I sat at
home and idly turned the pages of a new book Father
Agnew of St. Ignatius College had prepared for the
use of our catechists. Some words caught my eyes
and I resolutely shut the cover on the pages as
quickly as I could. When I recovered my poise I
continued to read:

> The Lord Jesus Christ is greatly more interested
> in the religious instruction of His little brethren
> than you are, Mister or Miss Catechist, who
> have generously and for love of Him undertaken
> to impart it. Your efforts are linked directly
> to the blessed labors of His own divine mission.
> The efficiency of your endeavors depends en-
> tirely upon the Divine grace with which He chooses
> to second them. The manner of His life and death
> is warrant aplenty that this necessary aid of His
> grace will never be wanting to you. The absence
> of any evidence of good effected by your efforts is
> no more a sign that your labors are barren of
> good results than were the multitudinous disap-
> pointments of the Master and His preaching and
> teaching a sign that His mission was a failure.

Mother happened into the library that night as I
sat with Father Agnew's booklet in my hand. She
had been late at the mission and should have been
tired, but suddenly she looked her old bright self
again. And I understood the reason, for the first

time in weeks I had been smiling. My decision had been made.

"What have you been busy with all afternoon, my dear?" she asked. "Presents?"

"I was with Catherine Jordan, mother," I replied. "One of the Jesuit scholastics brought these booklets by Father Agnew and we mailed them to all the catechists for Christmas."

"I got mine in the mail at the mission," said mother. "The booklet is truly excellent. Father Agnew is a grand man and a good priest to go to all that trouble."

"I think so, mother," I said quietly. "At least he has helped me make up my mind."

Mother's face clouded swiftly again. "What do you mean, Mary?" she asked.

"I have been talking things over with Catherine Jordan, mother," I said. "We've both decided you're so tired lately and the mission needs someone there to relieve you, and we should like to be the permanent residents."

She sat down, reached for a fan nearby, though it was winter, and fanned herself briskly. "I never heard of such nonsense," she said. "The likes of you and Catherine Jordan living there all alone. I'll never give my permission."

"Father will," I stated, none too confidently.

"Not if I see him first," she retorted.

I went to her and kissed her dear face. "Mother, you smiled when you came in, and I know why. For the first time in weeks you did not feel worried about me, and now you are beginning to worry all over again."

She sat still for a while weeping quietly; then we both got up and went to her little oratory. "I won't reside on Forquer Street," I reminded; "I would share Catherine Jordan's apartment in St. Francis School."

"It is a preposterous arrangement," mother stated after we had prayed for guidance. "I'll never agree to it. And for you to think of it, Mary, of all persons."

"Why not, mother," I answered eagerly. "Everyone agrees that the mission needs permanent residents to realize its full potential. I have understudied you a lot; and while I can't ever take your place, I feel I might help. It will be good for Catherine and me. You see, mother," I added with some mischief, "neither of us is as young as we used to be."

She blinked her eyes, as if she took in the full import of what I meant. "No matter," she commented angrily. "I will never agree to the arrangement, Mary, never."

But she did. Catherine and I arranged one of the large classrooms in the St. Francis School for a four-room apartment. The partitions ran head high like those used in the cheaper lodging houses in the neighborhood. But with Catherine's unfailing good humor and kindness and with the aid of a few things we bought or had freighted from our former homes, we soon had new quarters yielding the semblance of home.

I had made the great decision on December 25, 1913 but feared my decision to leave home on that date might never be explained on the score of the Christ Child. I expected a newspaper report. When I read the Chicago Tribune's caption, "Miss Mary Amberg Leaves Home of Wealth for Slum Work-- Will Quit Home of Ease to Live in Ghetto," I laughed and laughed. For me it was no such a thing. At last I was among my children. For the first time I felt that I really belonged.

I should go into detail, if space permitted, about Christmas 1914 at Guardian Angel Mission. Not because it was my first Christmas as resident or because mother still looked askance at the idea, but because the world was changing. In the dark war clouds hovering over Europe another terrible world was being born. I think because we and our Italian Americans sensed some of this, the Christmas of 1914 was deliberately made one of the happiest of our lives. All the blessed personages of the Christmas crib were permanent fixtures. We should therefore have been fairly familiar with the bambino and the madonna and St. Joseph, the shepherds, the wise men, the ox and the donkey, the sheep, and all the other figures attendant upon the birth of Christ. Yet never had the bambino looked more appealing. Never had the madonna seemed more beautiful. Never had good St. Joseph been of more noble mein. The alumnae and the students of the Academy of the Sacred Heart, Lake Forest, the girls from other academies and high schools, all our friends, and especially the Christ Child--all contributed to making it one of the most perfect Christmases ever at Holy Guardian Angel Mission.

The first year in which Catherine Jordan and I were permanent residents of the mission was also notable because it brought my dear friend Marie Plamondon oftener into our midst. The actual circumstances of her arrival were simple and reasonable enough. All of us who had known Marie as a tireless deb and expert horsewoman had never believed that among her many virtues was that of domesticity. I remember that shortly before Catherine and I had established ourselves as permanent residents of the mission, Marie had descended upon us with the family car full of stepladders, brooms, buckets, and soap powders too numerous to mention. "She washed the windows as if she were a union window washer," announced one of our children. "And you ought to see her painting the doors," added another.

While Catherine and I marveled over this newest evidence of Marie's universal talent the piece de resistance was yet to come. She had coaxed navy beans and a recipe from one of the women who had dropped in during the day, she informed us, and was nearly ready to introduce us to a perfect Friday dinner in the shape of some real Italian spaghetti. With considerable pride she showed us the recipe:

> 1/2 pound navy beans, previously soaked overnight
> 1 pound spaghetti
> 1/2 can tomato paste
> 2 onions, diced
> 1 spoonful olive oil
> 1 bay leaf
> Romano cheese

Catherine and I permitted ourselves to be led toward the kitchen of our little apartment. Over the top of the frame partitions, through the fumes of the fresh paint, came an odor that was not linseed oil nor turpentine but was immeasurably more pungent than both. When Marie opened the kitchen door, we exchanged the glances of martyrs ready to accept the worst. We realized that instead of sprinkling the cheese atop the spaghetti after it was on the serving platter, Marie had cooked the Romano in with the spaghetti. Our little apartment smelled like a goat farm.

"It's such a hot night, I think we all should go out to dinner," I suggested.

Marie took the assault on her Italian cookery like

a good soldier and began coming oftener to the mission, taking time from her numerous social affairs to see how it clicked, as she expressed it. As a very practical-minded person, she seemed baffled by our mission and housekeeping economics. I tried to explain that this was a world of varied interests: some civic-minded millionaires supported medical research, some financed the university training of the men and women of the future, and some supported ventures like Holy Guardian Angel Mission. To all of which Marie replied, "Rats!"

I had nothing to conceal from Marie. She was my lifelong friend. She had known the impulse behind my first association with mother in her activities at the mission. She had sensed something of my turmoil when I finally made the decision to reside permanently at the mission with Catherine. It appalled her, I think, that such a decision could have been made without any accompanying plan. Marie knew all or nearly all our patrons by name. She could deduce from our limited benefit affairs approximately how much money the mission received from those sources. And, while we had been blessed with a multitude of unselfish coworkers, they weren't enough. Marie, Catherine, and I had a long discussion about the mission's finances with our old friend Mr. Bogan. Marie had the account sheets for the past years. She also had the projected figures for next year's budget. None of the figures was very encouraging. Mr. Bogan finally said, "I have come to the same conclusion as Miss Plamondon, that if the mission is to carry on, you ought to form an auxiliary."

Mother and father did not like the idea, nor did I. Yet when we analyzed it, we saw that the idea was right and we were wrong. We were like the fond Latin mother who persists in carrying her bambino long after it should have been taught to walk by itself. What had first been conceived as a Christian duty by mother and her aides had expanded into a social program and produced civic advantages that were a credit to Chicago. We had acquired an ever-widening number of friends and well-wishers, and it was only fair to them that they should be given official recognition and a sense of responsibility in the affairs of the mission. We planned to offer five hundred ten-dollar auxiliary memberships. The resulting five thousand dollars would be used as a permanent fund for the maintenance of the mission.

Our tireless friend, Mr. William J. Bogan, called the auxiliary meeting to order in the Auditorium Building in 1915. All our friends had been very busy with good effect; for on the speakers' rostrum were Bishop A. J. McGavick of Holy Angels Church; Reverend Frederic Siedenburg, S.J., dean of the School of Sociology, Loyola University; Harriet Vittum, head resident of the Northwestern University Settlement; Judge Edward E. Brown, former justice of the Appellate Court; Mrs. Leonora Z. Meder, head of the social service agencies of Cook County; Professor W. H. Cahill, dean of the School of Engineering, Loyola University; Dr. A. De Roulet and M. F. Gurten; not to forget my mother and father, Marie's mother and father, and others.

I knew that all our friends and well-wishers were there for the purpose of securing continuing material assistance for the mission. But I was also drawing from the meeting quite another comfort for my morale. For when all was said and done, ours was a religious social settlement, not a purely secular one; and the presence of Bishop McGavick and Father Siedenberg combined to give our mission an importance I had always wanted it to possess. On the other side of the balance were my dear friends Harriet Vittum, Mrs. Meder, and Judge Brown. I felt our little mission had come a long way indeed from its first beginnings. Its possibilities were important enough to attract these outstanding figures in the religious, civic, and social life of Chicago.

Mr. Bogan introduced the speakers and presented his listeners with a brief resume of the mission activities. He emphasized the fact that in addition

to the Italian Americans the mission also served
other racial groups in our area. After his brief exposition, Mr. Bogan introduced Bishop McGavick,
the main speaker, who cited social settlement work
as an aid to spiritual activity. He stated that Catholics
had the moral obligation to support such work. He
stressed that every Catholic club or association
should not devote itself to social activity alone but
have an active interest in some form of charitable
endeavor. He closed his address with the hope that
the time would come when every parish and club in
the archdiocese of Chicago would be able and willing
to contribute to a cause as worthy as Holy Guardian
Angel Mission.

Miss Harriet Vittum, head resident of the Northwestern University Settlement, next addressed the
meeting. She spoke of the need for social settlements
as centers of civic welfare from which radiated all
manner of good, especially to the foreign-born,
foreign-speaking citizens who were the Americans
of the future. She referred to our mission as a
"switchboard" into which could be plugged all the
calls for help from the entire neighborhood. She gave
specific instances where aid had been received simply because a social settlement had been able to
organize the people into demanding their rights from
the city. "Incalculable good," remarked Miss Vittum,
"may be done by the social settlement in the area of
recreation alone. Upon nearly every street corner
is a saloon, a cheap dance hall, or a theater of
doubtful character, which a 'beneficent' city permits
for the entertainment of its young. And to fight these
we have only the social settlement. What welcome
conveniences it places before these young minds
craving a little pleasure and recreation. The homes
of settlement children are squalid tenement houses,
at best so overcrowded that any pleasant recreation
after a day of toil must of necessity be found away
from them. So the pleasure the social settlement
gives is really re-creation."

Father Siedenburg then took the floor. This great

Jesuit established the first school of sociology in any American university. He stated the need to place our mission on a sound financial basis to ensure that the work would continue. He cited the social settlement as one of the greatest influences in bettering the under-privileged and told how our mission had helped thousands of people to higher standards of living. Father Siedenburg then informed the gathering that their meeting was the first in a campaign to secure individual pledges of ten dollars a year from auxiliary members. The governing body of Holy Guardian Angel Mission would be selected from the donors, thus giving the public an opportunity to share in the work.

Next came Professor W. H. Cahill, dean of the School of Engineering of Loyola University. He had lived some years in Italy and gave a brief and interesting travel talk which was calculated to acquaint our listeners with various facets of the Italian-American temperament. Mrs. Leonora Z. Meder, head of the social service agencies of Cook County, next spoke of the inspiration to be derived from a visit to our mission and her personal knowledge of the civic service done there. Miss Adelaide Walsh, president of the Social Service Club and superintendent of the Children's Memorial Hospital, dwelt upon the untiring devotion and self-sacrifice of those who had begun and carried on the work of Holy Guardian Angel Mission. Dr. De Roulet spoke from a physician's viewpoint about the work done by our mission since he became interested in the Italian-American neighborhoods of Chicago. He also promised to look after all the medical needs of the mission free of charge.

Looking back I think the keynote of the appeal was sounded by Judge Brown. He finished his speech with a verse from "The Vision of Sir Launfall":

Not what we give, but what we share, -
For the gift without the giver is bare;
Who gives himself with his alms feeds three -
Himself, his hungering neighbor, and Me.

At the conclusion of the meeting an organizing committee was appointed with Bishop McGavick, honorary chairman; Father Siedenburg, active chairman; Mr. John A. Lynch of the National Bank of the Republic, treasurer; and Mr. Charles A. Gardiner, secretary. The committee decided upon a quick campaign for funds. The plan was for the committee to form a subsidiary committee of sixty persons, each of whom would contribute ten dollars and persuade ten other persons to contribute a like sum. If successful, this would realize $6,600.00, instead of the hoped for $5,000.00. The campaign consisted in sending out a report of the meeting and a letter written and signed by Father Siedenburg. We were fortunate that the Chicago newspapers had fully publicized the meeting and the ten-dollar subscriptions began to arrive in gratifying amounts. Dr. A. De Roulet and Dr. John A. Suldane began regular visiting days at the mission. Of the fifty-two settlement workers at the mission at that time all were volunteers. Neither I nor my coresidents Catherine Jordan, Margaret McGivern, and Don Kearins drew any salary. All the funds of the campaign committee would be turned over to the conduct of the mission and the welfare of those we served.

There is no need for me to mention more than briefly
the appalling sinking of the Lusitania on May 7, 1915.
The waves of that fatal shipwreck reached out to
engulf many lives among whom was my dear friend
Marie Plamondon whose father and mother lost their
lives aboard the great vessel. After hearing of her
parents' death Marie withdrew into the companionship
of her two sisters, Mrs. Allen Ripley and Mrs. J.
Henry Smith at Mount Pleasant Villa. Her older
brother Charles and younger brother Harold usually
accompanied father and mother and me when we went
there for weekend visits. I found that Marie had under-
gone her ordeal unusually well.

All of us were pleased when Marie returned from
the villa and reopened the family's townhouse at 2716
Lakeview Avenue with a tea for the Alliance Francaise
to supply medicine and knit goods for the allies. Marie
plunged anew into social affairs. Newspaper photographs
of her at this time show her at her best; sorrow had
sculpted here and there to bring the height of attractive-
ness and magnetism to her dear face. Only one who
knew her as well as I did could look beyond the mask
and sense the restlessness in her. Marie had taken
on so many social obligations under a certain compulsion
to be active. Though she enjoyed the love and companionship of her two fine sisters and brothers and a host
of relatives, Marie was frightfully lonely. Her kindred
had their own concerns and homes, whereas Marie
was unmarried. She could not see that this had perhaps
been providential and that it was little by little cutting
her away from the social life she had known. Nevertheless, while I strove to comfort Marie in every way

Marie Plamondon

I could, I never suggested anything openly to her. I simply devoted a greater part of my night prayers that God would lighten her burden.

Fortunately the pressure of my own work at the mission was such that I did not have much time for sorrow or worry or introspection. I find in my diary a copy of a program of the Guardian Angel's Center Benefit at Powers Theater, April 18, 1916. Marie Mayer, the Mary Magdalene of the Oberammergau passion play lectured on "The Message of the Passion Play." Music by well-known artists preceded the lecture. Tickets for the musical and lecture were one dollar each and the theater was filled.

The United States was fast approaching its own baptism in the inferno of the First World War. But for us at the mission there were a few festive oc-

casions that calmed our worries and fears. Shortly
after Miss Mayer's lecture in 1916, father and
mother entertained more than a hundred teachers
and workers of the mission at an old-fashioned May
supper with a reception afterward. The long tables
were laden with silver and crystal and delicious
food. All the places were bright with roses and the
gleam of pink candles while E. J. Fox in a happy little speech introduced Father Siedenburg. We were
always glad to have father with us; he made us feel
important and useful. Father Joseph Phelan, assistant pastor at Holy Name Cathedral where many
of us were parishioners, was also there. And I have
since thought that he did more for the material good
of the mission that day than all of us put together.

I did not know until long afterwards that Father
Phelan had been driven home by my friend Marie,
and that after eyeing her intently for a long while he
said, "The same old Marie, finer and deeper,
perhaps, for a little sorrow."

"Says you!" gibed Marie.

He patted her shoulder. "You haven't changed
much from the little girl I knew, Marie, but time
flies. Forty-one starts the downward slope, the
last half of our lives. The point is, Marie, what
are we all doing with our lives?"

Marie denies such a conversation, categorically.
She tells me that Father Phelan must have been talking in his sleep. On being cornered as to what he
actually did say, she will admit that perhaps he
asked her, "Marie--father gone, mother gone--what
are you going to do with your life?"

With the entry of the United States into the First
World War in 1917, Marie's older brother Charles
entered the officers' training school at Plattsburg
and her younger brother Harold was soon on his way
to France with the American Expeditionary Force.
Not to be outdone, Marie enrolled in the Bureau of
Water Corps Service here in Chicago. I am told that
after a short period of training she was able to take
apart an automobile faster than any expert, and what

is more, put it back together so it would work again. Her new duties were useful, needed, and gave patriotic women folk a sense of being wanted for war duty. Because of her innate sincerity, patriotism, and capacity for expression, Marie was much in demand as a public speaker. She really was several minutemen in one!

Those days after our country's entry into the First World War were trying ones for mother and me at the mission. Ironically though, in 1917 we received the largest funding from community Tag Day proceeds ever. But extraordinary expenses immediately appeared to offset the intake. In 1917 we added a Red Cross Auxiliary to our other activities. When the war was over it was heartening to hear from American Red Cross headquarters that Guardian Angel Mission had always scored high on the quality of bandages and other supplies.

And all this time our boys were going. Jack Landalo and James Morganelli were inducted into the army through the Students' Army Training Corps of St. Ignatius College. Roland Libonati received a commission as second lieutenant at the University of Michigan, Ann Arbor. Charles Gardiner had left his studies at De Paul, entered the Seventh Regiment in which his brothers were already enlisted, and was at Camp Houston. Oliver and Cyril Ward, my cousins, were among Guardian Angel's many alumni who answered their country's need. James Don Kearins, another of our mission workers, volunteered for ambulance duty in France.

Twenty odd years after the First World War ended our country and the world are in the throes of another war. As I look back I must admit that the popular mind of soldiers, sailors, and civilians in 1918 was more feasible, more easily focused, than in these later times. Our young men, seeing the last war's failure to achieve certain lofty democratic ideals, have grown more canny and circumspect. But the age-old pain and anguish of parental separation differs not one whit.

The First World War had its effect upon the activities of Guardian Angel's Center and brought us additional worries and concerns. Mother, father, and all of us had lulled ourselves into the thought that however imperfect its accommodations might be the Newberry Street location at least had the element of permanence. But this was not to be. Just as we had been asked to relinquish the classrooms at Holy Guardian Angel School in 1905, so now the archdiocese asked us to leave the rooms we occupied in St. Francis of Assisi School. The rooms we used for Guardian Angel's Center were to revert to use as a parish school. This would necessitate our finding new living quarters also; and if that were not feasible, an entirely new mission site.

The notice came to us early in 1917 from Archbishop Mundelein through the superintendent of Catholic schools. We felt that in many ways the notice was summary and unfair, but as loyal sheep of the flock we set out to obey the pastoral order. Our friends and supporters who thought we were not being fairly dealt with asked us to make representations to the archbishop. But this sort of reaction was contrary to mother's concept of Christian meekness and obedience. There was nothing for mother and all of us to do but to meet the conditions of removal which made it necessary to vacate our quarters in St. Francis School by mid-August 1917.

We all began a search for a suitable location. I placed my portion of the search under the guidance of St. Anthony, not only to help me secure a new home, but to enable us all to find a new site for our social settlement. Mother trusted implicitly in Our Lady of Perpetual Help. Catherine Jordan and Marie Plamondon likewise made novenas asking the intercession of their saintly namesakes in our common dilemma. Although we canvassed the neighborhood, there did not seem to be a suitable building in the entire Italian-American settlement. Archbishop Mundelein offered us a vacant lot in the neighborhood if we agreed to raise the funds necessary to erect a building for the mission. All of us felt that conditions called for a specially designed mission structure.

When the offer was announced at a board meeting, one of the directors had tentative plans for a building that could be erected for about fifty thousand dollars. It seemed an overwhelming amount to father, mother, and every one of us. Nevertheless there was cause for optimism. At the board meeting called to consider action on the plan, pledges totaling five thousand dollars were made by those in attendance and subsequently checks for an additional thirty-six hundred dollars came in for the building fund. Our canvassing for additional funds coincided with the United States' entry into World War I. Because our friends were now subjected to their own demands and expenditures, and because the costs of labor and material were soaring, the board decided to invest its eighty-six hundred dollars in liberty bonds for the duration of the war. I agreed because neither father, mother, nor any of us at the mission had been wholly in accord with the idea of a new building. The scheme was too grandiose. The facade might alienate the very people we wished to invite.

In my notebook for 1917 I find that we were operating above the normal record. Four children had been placed in dependable foster homes that we had secured after much investigation. Thirty-nine older boys had been assisted in finding jobs. At Christmas one hundred baskets of fruit had been distributed and 2,238 bags of candy, fruit, and toys had been given to the children of the Sunday school classes. With the advent of winter our relief committee had made over four hundred investigations and 171 destitute families were now on our relief roster. Every Sunday saw some mission club or sodality turning out for holy communion. Of our volunteer workers, three fine young men, Messrs. Boners, Ward, and Shoke, had become seminarians. Don Kearins would also have gone with them but was delayed because he had volunteered to go abroad with an ambulance unit.

While mother looked for a new location, she realized how hard it would be to move Guardian Angel's Social Center to another site. The physical aspects of moving were enormous. The kindergarten, the evening school, the sewing rooms, and the clubs of the social center served thousands of young and old. Five hundred items of clothing would have to be sent home partly finished with the girls who had sewn them. Mothers who had come to us for prenatal information, baby care, and nutritional advice would have to be contacted and given the name and address of a possible new location.

Meanwhile the friends of the mission took stock of the situation, the teachers divided themselves into search groups and investigated all possible sites. Our people besieged St. Anthony with novenas, insisting that he find a new location for the center and its staff.

I remember coming back to Chicago after one of my perennial health trips and accompanying mother and my sister Genevieve and Catherine Jordan on one of their reconnoitering expeditions. We went crisscross up and down the neighborhood without finding one prospective location. The only building which was at all suitable was the old Bremner mansion at 718 Loomis Street. It had been owned by the father of David F. Bremner, Jr., and the mansion had been disposed of by the family when the neighborhood began to change. The property consisted of a large two-story brick house, yard, and barn, and there was a smaller two-story residence to the north. Since the elder Bremner's death the proud old property had changed hands three times and was now owned by an influential and prosperous Italian American named Lespina, owner of L'Italia and reputedly a member of the Capone syndicate. When mother sought an interview with Mr. Lespina concerning the property, he told her he had no intention of selling it but planned to remodel the place and occupy it himself.

We had to turn our backs upon the attractive old

Mr. and Mrs. David F. Bremner, Sr., around 1915.

The Bremner home, 718 South Loomis Street, on the left, before 1900.

mansion and begin the search anew. We all made novenas to St. Anthony, Our Lady of Perpetual Help, and to all the heavenly hierarchy. The search finally narrowed down to two vacant store buildings adjoining each other at 927-931 West Polk Street. The structures had long been in disrepair and had subsided into a chronic state of shabbiness.

Polk Street was a curiously drab thoroughfare etched in dark brown monotone. Dusty windows stared at the passerby. Polk Street was home to Greek, Italian, and Mexican immigrants. It was also the working location of many trades and professions. As a vein of the city's transportation it fastens to Hull-House at Halsted Street and then runs toward the Loop in a maze of prehistoric cobblestones and business houses.

Moving to the new site on Polk Street brought all sorts of material aid from the alumnae of the Academy of the Sacred Heart, Lake Forest, and friends and well-wishers generally. It had given mother an idea of what the mission could be if it were largely planned and functioned on the scale it deserved. The new location also made news, bringing new workers and new donations.

After Catherine Jordan, Marie Plamondon, and their aides had given our new quarters a coat of paint, mother sensed that for all the constricted space the mission was again making headway.

After eight weeks on Polk Street the mission was as completely organized as it had been before and adult education classes were expanded and flourishing. We resumed the printing of The Sunday Companion, a four-page mimeographed leaflet which spread the news of our large Sunday school and of all our other activities. We could now boast two social clubs for our young people, an athletic club for boys and a social club for working girls. We had a more than passable choir that could sing Stehli's "Mass of the Angels." I was pressed into service now and then to play the organ, and my old friends, Misses Engel and Kiernan, worked with

Mrs. William A. Amberg at Mackinac Island.

the sewing classes. Mother was always planning new minstrel shows and dances, the kind of social treats needed to forestall the attraction of less desirable activities in the neighborhood.

But these activities were not all. Father considered it one of his proudest privileges to attend upon the activities at the mission. He was the most manly of men, and I know that mother invited and admired his interest in the older boys. He had the faculty of making them proud to be what they were. As he was an immigrant himself, he was a living symbol of the hope of the immigrant and his prospects in the new country. On father's part, I had often heard him say that his visits to the mission enriched him also. He was always bringing his friends, notables in civic life, to this and that affair at the mission.

There is a tremendous moral support for youth to
know that its activities have the friendly interest of
an oldster whose position and character they know
and respect.

The letters from our boys away in World War I
were long and even if censored made interesting
reading. Any word from Chicago in reply would be
interesting to our lads at the front, but any letter
from mother would be doubly so. How she did it I
do not know. All her replies were written on her own
best stationery in her own careful hand, and each
letter was intensely personal. This was all the more
extraordinary, for in those days mother was beset
with extraneous duties from all sides, patriotic and
civic as well as religious.
Painstaking as her mission work was, it was shel-
tered. Mother craved action and I know she experienced
it vicariously in her letters from our boys at the front.
I am glad that mother wrote to the boys and that we in
turn saved many of their letters. In fact we have
enough of them to make a book. Because of lack of
space I print this one from James Don Kearins.

Somewhere in France   August 1918

Dearest Mother Amberg,

From the dugout right at the front this letter
is coming, a dugout where from early morn you
hear the whine of shots going over or coming
back. Where all day long the battle is on and the
wounded are brought in hour after hour. Where
by night you would think h--- itself was here
within the noises and fiercely flickering lights
of battle. It was from the top of our dugout that
I saw the beautiful old town of . . . burn after a
terrific bombardment. A sight I shall never forget. We have now been in frontline billets for six
days. We have marched with litters on our shoulders for three days carrying the wounded. It

rained three of the days and we marched knee-
deep in mud, in all hours of the night, the air
wicked with the sound and rush of shells, and one
never knew when the next one would hit home.
It seems funny to say it, but in times like the
present I seem absolutely to have no fear--for
myself. My one thought is for the wounded and
the pals helping me carry the litter. (I don't
want to brag, but I must say that most all the
Tommies are crazy to work with me!)

I had quite a scare the other night when a sixty-
pounder landed near enough to lightly hit the lad
marching right ahead of me. Six feet. The piece
of metal from the shell hit him in the arm and
almost cut it off. He will not lose it, however, I
was glad to hear the surgeon say. Much to my
own surprise after the thing happened I was at
his side instantly, giving first aid. Strange . . .
when it was all over I found myself alone and
crying, which was okay, being alone, as it is not
kosher to cry before soldiers. It might upset
them. Another night in the dugout, when one could
hear Jerry flying over us and dropping bombs with
our names on them, I blew out all the lights and
started to tell funny stories. Nevertheless I would
have to pause for a little while now and then, hold-
ing my breath fearfully, until I counted Jerry's
load. One, two, three, and so on. When the last
one dropped it would be all right . . . until the
next time.

So you see at last to my delight another from
old Guardian Angel's Center is doing his bit, and
in a part he loves. He tries his best to be cheerful at all times, remembering that dear old spot
of cheer and joy and the light that will burn for
his return, watching over him. I have told you
a few of the dangers and there are many. But
there are other things, too. The cool brave way
the wounded speak of "The Huns." The little tots
in the town hard by whom I tried to teach games,
and who had the time of their lives with me be-

cause they couldn't understand English nor could
I understand their French. But they knew the
games! Then the chaplain came along, speaking
beautiful French, and everything was hunky-
dory.

I had charge of a ward (seven tents) in the
town, and when I left it was to go forward at my
own request. Tears came to my eyes when I
heard all the nice things they said about me. The
Tommies stand a very real test: you like them
as well when they are sick as when they are well,
which is saying a lot. However, we are getting
more Yanks in billets around here right along,
and I am beginning to feel more at home. Wher-
ever the Yanks are they seem to bring and infuse
a new spirit. It is absolutely wonderful. I am very
proud of my countrymen, of everyone I see, more
and more. With myself it is the same old story
as it was with the Newberry boys. I am not
ashamed, either. When the bombs sing overhead
I put a bold face on and stick it out, even if I am
shaking like a leaf inside . . . and don't let anyone tell you he feels any different under fire.
Then when night comes on I lie deep in the dugout,
thinking of you, and wishing I were there with you
all, so we could hide behind the door as in the
old days and laugh when the others marveled
over my wonderful bravery.

I met a cocky little English R. C. chaplain
the other day, whose nickname among the soldiers
is Happy Face. He is not a bit good looking, but
he is always smiling and each time goes over the
top with his boys. He brings the hosts for holy
communion to us every day no matter how threat-
ening the Heinies are or how bad the weather or
how fierce the battle may be going for his boys.
Everyone calls him Father.

Everything went well lately. Very little wounded.
Living in a six-foot by five-foot dugout. Now coin-
cidence: The other day I was in a ward at the hospital, when all of a sudden I heard, "Excuse me,

please, Mr. Kearins; I know you!" I looked around
--and there stood Philip Spezia of 1007 Jefferson
Street and a member of our band. The characteristic way Philip had addressed me tickled everybody. All day long all I heard was, "Excuse me,
please, Mr. Kearins; I know you!" with all sorts
of inflections. (Not all flattering.)

Don Kearins

Answering all the war letters became quite a
problem until our worn old office mimeograph was
rehabilitated and put into service to print the Guardian Angel's Bulletin. It was a humble four-page affair, but it made up in affection, interest, and in-
tensity what it lacked in format and aesthetics.
   We all hoped and prayed that our boys might be
kept safe. Knowing the tragedy that had already
entered the lives of my dear friend Marie, her
brothers and sisters, I was not too sanguine that
we alone might be spared.
   We finally received word of Charles Gardiner's
death. He had given tireless service to Guardian
Angel Mission, first as catechist, then as a teacher,
and later as an aid when he passed his bar exam-
inations and had become an attorney. He had argued
many of our people's cases in court without any
thought of fees. He had volunteered for the officers'
training school at Fort Sheridan at the outbreak of
the war. But because he was weak as a result of a
recent operation, he had been refused. Then he
enlisted in the quartermaster's corps at Camp
Johnston where he was one of the victims of an outbreak of spinal meningitis. Because of the army
quarantine regulations his body was not brought beyond
the Illinois Central depot. Instead all of us journeyed
to Ascension Church in Oak Park for a solemn requiem
Mass. Father Quille of the Working Boys' Home was
the celebrant and Father F. X. Breen preached the
sermon. Father Breen had known Charles since his
student days at St. Ignatius College. After the Mass

we all went to the Illinois Central depot where a bugler sounded taps, an honor guard fired the last salute, and the flag of his country and our service flag were draped over the pinewood box that held the last of our valued friend and helper.

We had hardly recovered from the shock of Charles Gardiner's death when my cousin Oliver Ward was killed by a high-explosive shell somewhere in France on October 18, 1918. We were all so proud of Ollie, as we called him, and had hoped that he would have become an officer. His brother Cyril, also a sergeant, wrote us the details later. Ollie had been returning from the train headquarters to his own company's billet at the front when a shell landed on the tent, killing him instantly. Father Ahern, a chaplain, and Colonel Fisher, Ollie's superior officer, found the body and gave it temporary burial. Father Ahern said a Mass of the dead for Ollie's soul next morning. It was a great comfort for us to learn later that Ollie had gone to confession and communion only three days before his death.

Thanksgiving Day in 1918 began to take on more of its former aspect for us. Quite a few of our lads were now demobilized. By December 8, the feast of the Immaculate Conception, nearly all our boys were present in uniform at the solemn high Mass of thanksgiving celebrated in Holy Guardian Angel Church. A procession of thankful neighbors moved in and out of the church and the center all day. We had a little celebration in the evening. One of our workers had inscribed an honor roll and Father Francis X. Breen presented it to us on behalf of the men. The parents and friends of our boys were present and there were no dry eyes as Father Breen read the simple citations and service records of our boys. Everyone said that the dance that followed the entertainment was quite the jolliest the center had ever seen.

After demobilization we strove to help our boys integrate into civilian life again. Red Cross activities ended in our program. Though here and there spots of unemployment remained, our people were mostly employed and making better money and enjoying better living conditions than before. The mission itself had reason to rejoice that year of 1918, for we were now a duly accredited social settlement and were on the list authorized by the Chicago Charities. This meant that we were entitled to draw our allotment from the Community Chest, making our income for 1918 three hundred dollars more than we had enjoyed the year before.

But with inflation under way and prices skyrocketing, Marie Plamondon, Catherine Jordan, father, mother, and I went into a huddle on the matter of finances. We threshed matters out and decided to revive the idea of an auxiliary which had been dormant for some months due to the pressure of patriotic activities. Accordingly a committee was formed with this end in view. It included mother, Marie Plamondon, Catherine Jordan, Anna Cox, Mrs. F. J. Noonan, Stella L. Metzger, Marian Hallinan, Mabel Dorsey, Olive Collins, Katherine Cremin, Mrs. John O'Donoghue, Louise Wolf, Marion McGuire, and myself. The committee accepted Anna Cox's suggestion that we forget all past funding efforts as though they had never been and proceed to make the new auxiliary self-supporting on its own account.

The auxiliary was to meet monthly and Anna Cox asked me to have all the facts and figures together for the first meeting which was to be held on the night of January 19, 1919 in the Green Room of the Auditorium Hotel. The large attendance of our clerical and lay friends at the meeting was very encouraging. Mrs. Anthony J. Merrill presented the arguments in favor of our friends and patrons all becoming members of Guardian Angel's Auxiliary. At the close of her speech I made a brief statement of the aims and purposes of the proposed auxiliary and how it was to further the aims and interests of the mission. The annual dues of the auxiliary were to be only one dollar, and we hoped for each member's interest in our annual tea dances but also in the daily activities of the center.

At the close of the meeting Frances Walsh was named secretary pro tem, Mabel Theresa DeSmet and Frances McElroy were appointed members of a committee on constitution and bylaws with Mabel Dorsey chairman. It was not advisable to hold a regular election of officers until the plans for the auxiliary were better developed. I did appoint a committee on nominations to choose officers and directors until a regular election could be held. Mrs. Frances J. Noonan was made chairman of this committee, with Stella Metzger, Marian Hallinan, Marion McGuire, Olive Collins, Anna O'Neil, Louise Wolf, Katherine Cremin, and Mrs. John O'Donoghue as members. I also proposed that the meetings of the auxiliary should be held on the third Saturday of each month at some downtown meeting place for the convenience of the members.

Our second auxiliary meeting was therefore held on February 14, 1919 at the LaSalle Hotel. Mother was present but listless and tired. Anna Cox was also there, and as temporary chairman called the meeting to order and briefly recapitulated the purpose of the auxiliary. Marie Plamondon was there too, still in her uniform. Though World War I was over, she was serving through demobilization. It was a great relief to me and Marie and all of us when the committee moved to appoint Mrs. Anthony J. Merrill chairman of our auxiliary. Then as many times afterward she was our fairy godmother, even as Marie Plamondon became a sort of <u>dea</u> <u>ex</u> <u>machina</u>.

Marie's well-fitting grey serge jacket, her Sam Brown belt, her capacity for rendering a hearty "Damn!" when things did not go exactly right, all awed and impressed the younger male elements in our midst. Poor lads, little did they know that her heart was pure gelatine, and she would even have given them her Sam Brown belt if it meant adding anything to their happiness. They did not see the dark night of the soul that still existed for Marie as it once did for me. Marie did not hide many things from me, though she put up a brave front to everyone else. She was so lonely in spite of her two fine sisters, in spite of the joy of seeing her brothers demobilized and safe again at home. I finally gave up worrying about Marie's soul and concentrated anew upon my own and its problems. God's light had sought out and found her. I would be patient, cooperate in all ways with the work of the auxiliary, and leave everything to God to handle as he saw fit in his own good time.

World War I brought its complications to my father. The barrage of propaganda let loose by self-styled patriots against loyal citizens of German extraction was very cruel. Though at the beginning of the war father had been hale and vigorous and showed no outward sign of physical illness, I do know that brooding over unjustified attacks against German immigrants undermined his stout heart and endangered his health. Mother sensed this also. She relinquished all social activities and all extraneous duties to spend as much time as possible with father. The family spent the summer of 1918 together at Edgecliffe, our summer home on Mackinac Island. Neither mother, my brother, nor my sisters neglected any attention to let father know we loved him. But it was no use. The Death Angel had lain his hand upon that brow. Father was not bedridden. However, early in September there were a few hours of unmistakably severe illness. These gave us time to call a priest and have father given the last sacraments. Then he went to his reward.

The funeral was held from our family home at 1301 North State Street to Holy Name Cathedral on Monday, September 9, 1918. A solemn requiem Mass was celebrated in the presence of Archbishop Mundelein. The celebrant was our friend Bishop Dunne of Peoria. The assistant priest was Monsignor M. J. Fitzsimmons. Reverend Francis X. Breen, S.J., was deacon, and Reverend M. Cavallo, sub-

William A. Amberg, 1847-1918.

Edgecliffe, the Amberg home on Mackinac Island.

deacon. There were present in the sanctuary many
other of our priestly friends including Fathers Chenuil
and Ciufoletti of Holy Guardian Angel Church. Reverend Thomas F. Burke, C.S.P., of Old St. Mary's
Church preached the sermon. In the pews were a
delegation of the Madames of the Sacred Heart and
other nuns, representatives of every business and
social strata of the city. The pallbearers were men
who had grown up in the mercantile and civic life
of Chicago. Interment was in our family lot at Calvary
Cemetery where the Most Reverend Archbishop gave
the last absolution.

Mother bore up bravely through the succeeding
days. Though so beautiful had been her married life
with father, so well mated had they been, she weak-
ened visibly as one who had lost the better part of
her being. Yet she strove to carry on as usual, sub-
merging her own sorrow in deference to the needs
of others. It was fine and lovely of her to do so, but
we could see how greatly she had failed in health. It
was incomprehensible to me to see the change in the
active and energetic person who was my mother.
But the phenomenon was there, all who loved her
both saw and felt it. For years she had done the work
of three women. Her heart was expansive. It extended to all her people. Until I watched mother
pray and listened, I never fully learned what it meant
in the biblical phrase to pray without ceasing. "What
information can you give us of John Ianola who died
in the service?" was the sort of telegram mother
could speed to Washington on the very day after father's funeral. "Poor John," she said to us. "Let us
pray for his soul."

I was with mother all the time those days, and
all the former vitality was in her voice as she discussed this and that aspect of the center and its
service to our Italian-American people. She had
grown to be such a great and grand soul that she
found her chief pleasures those days in her treasure
of memories. She had fought the good fight. She had
kept the faith. And she had arranged that the same

faith would be nourished and rekindled in the hearts and souls of countless other people. For her I could only feel a most generous envy, knowing she was going to meet her Maker and render an account of her stewardship more nobly than any of us could hope to do.

She was actually impatient with the doctor's and nurse's kind attention. I remember the day that Father Fitzsimmons came to give her extreme unction. Her work at the center was done and she knew that Catherine, Marie, and I and all our helpers would carry on her ideas and hopes and plans insofar as we were able.

Mother did not rally after receiving the last sacraments. She prayed in thanksgiving for some time after the priest had gone, then she turned to me and said with a firm voice, "Mary, don't forget the homecoming dance for our boys." The honor roll was also uppermost in her mind. It was her last will and testament to safeguard and ensure the continuance of the center she loved. She died on November 14, 1919.

The recent loss of my father was overwhelming; yet I do not know any word to describe the emptiness and desolation I felt when my mother departed. Mother had at last attained her wish. His grace, Archbishop Mundelein, had given the final absolution. Her body lay in Calvary Cemetery beside my father. My sister, my brother, and I had to carry on.

I had long ago made my choice and I could not afford to indulge self-pity now. My mother had given me life, and I owed it to her to keep on giving my life to the project that had been so close to her heart.

From the time of their marriage in 1869, father and mother gave of themselves and their wealth and time and labor without stint for every worthy cause of Christ's Church and his vineyard. St. Vincent's Orphan Asylum owes much of its enviable status and reputation to my dear mother. Mother also filled several terms as president of the auxiliary formed to assist the Sisters of the Good Shepherd in their efforts for wayward girls. Among her own class-mates of the Academy of the Sacred Heart she was president, first of the Enfants de Marie, the Children of Mary Society, and later of the Alumnae Sodality. She was largely instrumental in the very year before her death in bringing to Chicago the Religious of the Cenacle, an order of nuns who facilitate women's retreats. It was one of the stark coincidences of life that Archbishop Mundelein, to whom she had presented the sisters of the Cenacle upon their arrival in Chicago, should within a few months be praying over her dead body the last absolution of the Church she served so well.

Madonna Center Moves
to Loomis Street, 1922

The work of Guardian Angel Mission continued on
Forquer Street and the social center provided its
numerous services from our Polk Street location.
Then one day newspaper headlines screamed that
Mr. Lespina had been murdered. It had long been
rumored that Mr. Lespina had been an aide of the
notorious D'Andrea, who in turn was said to be a
henchman of the equally notorious Al Capone. The
neighborhood was full of gossip that Sunday afternoon. My friends stood wide-eyed in the doorways
discussing this latest deed which had again brought
disrepute to their neighborhood. I said the Christian's
usual prayer for the man falling to an assassin's bullet
"Requiescat in pace!"

Imagine my astonishment in the wake of all this to
enter Holy Guardian Angel Church that Sunday and to
find Marie Plamondon sitting among our children's
choir in the organ loft! There she sat, her roguish
eyes glistening, her arms folded across her bosom,
her long limbs cramped within the confines of the
pew; and she looked more happy and cheerful than I
had remembered her for months. It was like the old
Marie we had all known and had all but forgotten.

"It is so nice to find you here, Marie," I said
quite matter-of-factly with an effort to conceal my
surprise. But I know my eyes asked, "What are you
doing here?"

"All I know is what I read in the newspapers,"
she rejoined, using Will Rogers' favorite counter-
point. Then she drew me down beside her and whispered, "I saw a newspaper extra about the assassi-
nation. I thought I'd better come over here and help

look after you and Catherine. Things have been happening fast, Mary, too fast for two unsophisticated girls like you and Catherine. The headlines about Lespina, and everything happening right on the sidewalk in front of Uncle David's house. When we get that house, Mary, I'm coming with you--to stay."

"To stay?" I repeated.

"I don't chew my cabbage twice," retorted Marie.

I pressed her hand. "Why that's fine, Marie; simply fine. As soon as Benediction is over we'll go shopping on Maxwell Street for a folding bed."

"I want none of your folding beds," she said with unwonted stubbornness. "Folding beds and tenements have brought about most of the evils in the city. I want a full size bed, my dear, or nothing."

"Then we'll certainly have to move," I said. "There isn't room where we are."

"Exactly what I've been saying, isn't it?" she scathed. "And that's why I am here. And maybe that's why Mrs. Lespina is down there," and she indicated the short, squat figure of a woman heavily swathed in black who knelt all but hidden on one side of the church surrounded by the children. I divined Marie's meaning instantly.

"Shall I tell Catherine and the others that you have come to join us permanently, Marie?" I asked her as I began arranging the music.

"I'll do it myself when I get ready," she answered.

Practical-minded, resourceful, aggressive Marie descended upon us with her bold plan in a time of trial and perplexity. It was the answer to long prayers. After Benediction the congregation gathered around the portico for visits and conversation. Some few friends went and consoled Mrs. Lespina; the majority respected her grief and let her alone. But when she saw Marie and myself leaving in the midst of our children, she came toward us.

"I saw you lots of times speaking to him and looking at the Bremner house," she said without more ado. "I will sell it to you, Miss Mary, cheap. For a song. I have lost my husband. I care for nothing now. Nothing, anymore."

We consoled and thanked her but made no promises. Money matters were out of our hands; the responsibility of purchase lay with the auxiliary. But before suppertime Marie and I fulfilled our promise to Mrs. Lespina that we would come and look over the premises so that we could make the proper recommendations to our board of directors.

Tenement fever had indeed fallen like a blight upon the once proud Bremner mansion. The basement was given over to an Italian-American grocery. The window was piled high with dried fish and squid, dried peppers, Italian cheeses and salami that made part of the window seem like a garden of gourds. Since we were known to many of the tenants and bore Mrs. Lespina's card, we were allowed to enter the premises. We did not peer through door cracks but contented ourselves in meandering along the lower corridor, then turning up the stairway from the paneled hall. On the landing Marie halted and sniffed. "Someone's cooking with Romano cheese, like the time my spaghetti dinner came a cropper," she said faintly. "No," she continued as we went on up the steps, "this isn't just Romano cheese cooking; it's the real McCoy!"

And indeed it was. For when we reached the front room upstairs which had been Mr. Bremner's library where my brother and sister and I had heard many a childish fairy story while seated on his lap, we heard the bleat of a goat and entering found an Angora nanny goat and two of her kids. She was quite tame and did not attempt to butt Marie out for this intrusion into her domain. I remained prudently at the door, watching Marie make her scornful round of the stable. One half of the room was thick with goat hair, and we did not doubt that children or adults might sleep upon it at night in this crowded tenement.

When I left the ancestral home of the Bremners with Marie, we walked back to Polk Street and my thoughts tinged with melancholy. Somehow my thought that the house could serve as a new site for the mission seemed unduly optimistic. I wondered why Mrs. Lespina had wished to sell us such an obviously profitable tenement. Strangely enough when Marie and I returned to the mission we found Mrs. Lespina awaiting us. She said that she feared we had not understood what she had told us when we met her outside church after vespers a few hours before. She could never bear to live near the spot where her husband had been slain, and she again offered to sell at a figure so reasonable and so well within our credit limitations that in spite of my melancholy I immediately became hopeful again. But I did not appear too eager, though I was very anxious to enter into negotiations for the Lespina property. The new site for the mission seemed necessary to establish Marie as a coresident with Catherine Jordan and myself.

Though we told Mrs. Lespina we should have to take the matter under advisement, Marie and I agreed that at last we had something tangible to suggest to our many friends and supporters. Accordingly I went to Anna Cox, the chairman of the auxiliary committee. She also agreed that our long-delayed hope was on the verge of blossom, and she sent invitations to our patrons and friends to attend a meeting to develop a plan to purchase the Lespina property. This was the tide which would crest us into the haven of our hopes.

The meeting would also determine the name by which our social settlement was thenceforth to be known. We had graduated from being known simply as the mission, then Holy Guardian Angel Mission, even St. Francis Mission. And now we would attain mother's final wish of having our location and our activities known as Madonna Center. The name Madonna was dear to mother and had many dear connotations for our people; Center indicated a gathering place, a focal point, a social force in the neighborhood.

The purchase of the new site included a two-story structure to the north of the one-time Bremner residence. This building would serve as the office and our residence. It was arranged to have the office downstairs and living quarters for myself and Marie Plamondon upstairs. When we finally completed the move to Madonna Center on Loomis Street, Bishop Dunne came from Peoria to bless our premises and be our guest at the inaugural reception.

What more is there to add, except that the Madonna for whom the settlement was named quickly made her beneficence known. For days carts and wagons and autos came along Loomis Street to our door and discharged a plethora of new and used furniture and furnishings. On the moving day the center buildings shone inside and out. All our people and our friends had taken a hand that all might be ready for Madonna Center's simple but efficient christening.

When we were at last settled in the old Bremner homestead, I came home one August day to our simple lodgings on the second floor above the office. Hearing a rustle of papers and a typewriter and knowing Catherine Jordan was not on duty, I halted within the hall door at the head of the stairs. There, seated at

Madonna Center, 718 and 712 South Loomis Street, Chicago, in 1940.

a tall mahogany secretary that I knew had been her mother's, sat Marie with her portable typewriter busy with papers.

"Oh," I breathed, my hand stilling my surging heart. "It's you!"

She did not even lift her head to look at me. Instead, "Who did you think it was?" came the ungracious snort of our new coresident. "Now don't stand there like a Maxwell Street dummy. Please shut the door and don't let in the flies."

Our new home on South Loomis Street did not look very much like a social settlement when we moved into it on that sunny day in January of 1922. For days previous all of us had been busy on the premises, working with might and main and laundry soap. I heard little Teresa tell Mario as they watched the unloading of the moving vans, "This ain't going to be no school. This is a sociable settlement."

When mother died my brother and sister and I agreed to close the house on North State Street and we made a division of our favorite pieces of furniture. Very little sufficed for me. The apartment I had ar-

Resident directors' living room, second floor, 712 South Loomis Street.

ranged to occupy with Catherine Jordan and Marie on
the second floor of 712 South Loomis Street was too
tiny to permit more than a few of the familiar old
belongings. The flat consisted of a living room, a
dining room, two bedrooms, a bath, and a front
alcove. In the latter we created a small oratory with
mother's favorite alabaster statuette of Our Lady of
Perpetual Help, her prie-dieu, and some potted
plants. The picture of the Madonna which still hangs
above the mantle in the front room of the settlement
was the first of our belongings to be placed in our
new home. When my former home on North State
Street was demolished, I retrieved some of the
Norton ebony and gold window trimming of the familiar old drawing room for the similar parlor of
the Bremners. Much of the woodwork in our new
location had been cut and chopped away by the tenants
in the winters when the place had been a tenement.
But actually in those first months of 1922, none of
us troubled too much about our living quarters. It
was a comfortable sort of place due principally to
Marie. I have never seen anyone with her particular
talent for improving cast-off furniture until it became something beautiful.

We had memories of our own bygone days in that
neighborhood. For though the neighborhood had de-
teriorated vastly, many of the houses looked much
as they did in the former years. From our front
windows I could look out in reverie and see the
wedding guests thronging in and out of the mansion
where my friend Mrs. Edward Hines had been married and where she had been such a joyous and un-
troubled bride. The Cummings, Moody, Gordon,
and Corboy mansions were outwardly much as they
were before, all visible from our windows.

Unlike these mansions, however, which had been
built close up to by the adjoining tenements on either
side, our new home still had the merit of spacious-
ness and light all around. It consisted of the large
mansion on the corner, 718 South Loomis, surrounded
with sufficient space for a playground. It was spacious

Madonna Center, front parlor, 718 South Loomis Street.

Madonna Center, front parlor looking east, 718 South Loomis Street.

enough within for classrooms, playrooms, library, club rooms, attendants' office, and kitchen. The smaller building immediately to the north, 712 South Loomis, was the one we occupied for office and living quarters. The stable and carriage house we gradually converted into a gymnasium with the up-stairs made over for living quarters. This sudden projection into surroundings far more ample than any location we had used before was not an unmixed blessing. We suddenly felt like the two-room family inheriting an overwhelmingly spacious estate. At the same time we had the satisfying feeling that for the first time since mother and her friends had founded the settlement which Madonna Center had become we had a prospect grand and vast enough for any amplitude and variety we could give our plans, if we only had the money. This the auxiliary under-took to supply. But even that did not seem to matter. We were all so happy at the center those days, res-idents, teachers, children, grown-ups, that God's blessing seemed to be over all; and we could have gone ahead cheerfully even if our larder and our treasury were empty.

Madonna Center, looking northeast from Lexington Street, 1948.

Boys at Madonna Center, 1940.

    # The Services of Madonna Center

At Madonna Center every inch of space serves many purposes. We begin with our prekindergarten class. The average weekday attendance here at Madonna Center is about sixty children. The preschool classroom is a very pleasant place with its east, south, and west exposures, its wee chairs and other furnishings painted in bright colors. The crackers and milk for class intermission are served by the children to each other. We strive to give our children a sense of the joy and dignity of serving one another. The prekindergarten class opens with prayer. Our children pass from our care to both the parish and the public school. We strive to lay a groundwork of adherence to the faith which our children will carry with them all their lives. Our pedagogical technique is modern and most appropriate to the needs of the children. It was originally formulated with the aid of William J. Bogan, later superintendent of Chicago's public schools.

While other nationalities are represented, Italian Americans predominate in the children attending our prekindergarten. Most of our children come from poor homes, from immigrant parents who are uneducated by American standards.

Every child at Madonna Center is examined by a doctor. If necessary, we see to it that the child receives the required medical treatment. We also have a branch of the Elizabeth McCormick Memorial Fund which comes to the center two or three times a week to work for undernourished children. We also conduct nutrition classes for the mothers of our children in the prekindergarten class and send out our social workers to follow up particular cases.

There was and always is much pleasure in teaching our tots. With immigration now practically at a halt, it must not be forgotten that for one child that is now taught English there was a time when there were two that required to be taught to speak it. Let me take the case of Mario, one of the many children in our group of five-year-olds in 1925. One look at that petulant, finely molded face tells his teacher that here is no patterned individual but one with strongly marked predilections. As the only boy in a family of father, mother, and five daughters, Mario has been spoiled. To deflect his self-interest into gregarious channels and make him sociable with youngsters of his own age would be enough of a task without trying to teach him a new language.

I knew that our angel-faced Mario was about to upset the class and that too much chiding might be

Prekindergarten class with Nell O'Brien, 1940.

disastrous. Our instructor went about things in another way. "This is Mario Comito," she told his
classmates. "He has come to America on a big boat
across the ocean from Italy. He came from New
York on a big train to live in Chicago. As yet he does
not speak the way we do; but he wishes to, very much.
He wants to say 'Good morning!' instead of 'Buon'
jiorno!' Won't you all say "Good morning' to Mario?"

When Mario came to class again next morning his
teacher said, "buon' jiorno . . . Good morning,
Mario!" and the class repeated the greeting. He was
shown to his chair and the teacher explained very
carefully the name and use of the crayons, paper,
pencil, and sketching models in Italian as well as in
English. Later his classmates would help Mario
name and find what he wanted. He strove manfully to
remember the English words the children and the
teacher told him. Children are very imitative and
want to be a part of a sympathetic group. All that
second day in kindergarten his teacher remained
close beside Mario. Mario learned that his adjustment to the group, however difficult, was something
that he could accomplish through the use of English
words. Mario was given alphabet blocks, a simple
reader and speller, and he soon found a harmonious
playmate who came from a household where everyone
spoke English. In two weeks Mario could express himself fairly well in one-word English.

Our children came to realize as their classwork
progressed and they made new playmates at the center
that many peoples and races had contributed to America
growth and made Chicago the great American city it has
become. It was a never-failing source of delight to
see the many spiritual bouquets our children would offer us and our benefactors. I might add that a spiritual bouquet consists of prayers, good works, holy
communions, self-denials, and penances which one
does as spiritual acts of mercy. The giver of the bouquet offers them to God for the spiritual welfare of
the recipient. Here is a typical spiritual bouquet. I
find it in my scrapbook dated January 3, 1923.

My dearest Miss Mary,

We, the Agnes Ward Amberg Communion Guild, are sorry that you could not attend our meeting today. We are giving you a blessed candle to be kept at the center to be used for its purposes and on the feast days. We girls are going to communion tomorrow for Florence Cremin, your little niece. Some girls are going to make a novena by going to communion every morning, and some are making prayer novenas. Hoping that God will restore her to health and strength very soon. Dear Miss Mary, we who are named in honor of your sainted mother never forget you and all our teachers in our prayers and communions and we will remember you and your special intentions during Lent. May God bless you always.

> Agnes Ward Amberg Communion Guild
> Mary Filichio, President
> Josephine Butellotti, Secretary

Children at Madonna Center.

Anyone who helps a child to integrate himself as a personality into the work of this world renders a service which is very important. When one deals with children it is also important to know their parents. Hygiene taught in kindergarten was followed up in the childrens' homes. Miss Mack, our visiting nurse, was so insistent upon the merits of soap and water and so well endowed with mental and physical powers that she is usually able to put her principles and orders into instant effect. There is a Loomis Street tradition which has it that even the sight of Miss Mack coming along the street is sufficient to send an entire household rushing headlong toward the kitchen sink crying, "Here comes soap and water!" This was her nickname for a long time until our people came to know Miss Mack better and to appreciate her other qualities and unfailing good humor. Such neighborhood visiting is vital and has always been a characteristic of Madonna Center.

Due to the penny milk program we do not encounter as many cases of malnutrition among our underprivileged children as we used to. But vitamin deficiencies are numerous enough to continue to be a disturbing factor. The percentage of four- and five-year-olds who are rickety, whose teeth literally fall out under the visiting dentist's examination, has fortunately become less and less. In extreme cases we always manage to find ways of supplying orange juice and milk quickly, lots of it, and for as long a time as is necessary. One gains a sort of diagnostic sixth sense when dealing with underprivileged tots.

It is often discouraging to give a list of food suggestions to the mother of undernourished little ones, only to find one's suggestions not followed. Italian Americans cling tenaciously to such native staples as spaghetti, macaroni, tomato pulp, olive oil, vino tinto, certain Italian legumes, and Italian bread. The bread, like the spaghetti and macaroni, is of durum wheat flour and better than that made from

ordinary white flour. The Italians have always supplemented and balanced their protein diet with a
great variety of greens and vegetables. Endives
and broccoli, long favorite Italian greens, have
become commonplace on the American table.
Whereas our grandmothers always strove to have
dandelion greens in the spring "to thin the blood"
after a long winter, our Italian Americans eat a
cultivated variety of dandelion greens the year round.
The Italian-American taste for cheese is likewise
traditional.

Our workers and family visitors do not attempt to
upset a family's familiar bill of fare; it would be
foolish to attempt to do so. If the family is not too
poor, the mother always manages to prepare an ap-
petizing and nourishing meal out of familiar Italian
ingredients. Our workers know that Italian Americans
as a rule possess healthier hair and teeth than the
majority of their fellow citizens. They are fiercely
proud of their offspring and wish to do everything
they can to further their health, the comfort of their
surroundings, home sanitation, and children's prospects in life.

One frequently encounters the case of the employed mother whose income is necessary to sup-
lement that of her husband. She may have to work
because the husband is incapacitated. St. Ann's Day
Nursery is maintained for these people. We give
very young children and babies the usual clinical tests
to ensure good health. Those who are old enough are
allowed to attend the kindergarten class. We make
no fixed charge for taking care of the children placed
in our charge. We discuss matters with the mother
and consider her viewpoint in working out a plan of
care. In the majority of cases no charge is made.

We hold regular clinics for prenatal care. For
many years our people have enjoyed the services of
some of Chicago's best obstetricians and physicians,
Dr. John Suldane and others. Of course such a staff
is woefully small for the work it has to do and could

Dr. John Suldane

do. Birth control propaganda has penetrated our underprivileged neighborhoods through misnamed evangels who fail to realize that it were better for our country to encourage the prolific and substantial Italian-American parentage rather than to attempt to dam such valuable fecundity at its sources. Were it not for our volunteer workers, we could not checkmate as much of this unpatriotic and biologically false propaganda as we do. Many of our current staff workers in the prenatal clinic are from Loyola University. In the nursery many helpers are domestic science and sociology students from Mundelein College. We are grateful for the help they give.

Sewing and Domestic Science Classes

I have always viewed Madonna Center as an oasis in
the midst of the city. There is still a vast difference
in the life our young people can live in Madonna
Center and their existence away from it. Living
conditions have improved only too gradually in the
neighborhood as the years have passed. There is
now a more pleasant homelife in better furnished
flats than heretofore.

After the kindergarten we teach the girls domestic science, baby hygiene, and plain and fancy sewing.
The boys are divided into baseball and football teams,
and a complete gym program suited to their growing
bodies is provided to train their muscles and make
them strong. Meanwhile there are hikes for both
boys and girls. There are visits to parks, museums,
zoos, and other Chicago and suburban places of
interest on the calendar. The children all bring
their own lunches if they can. If not, the hike leader
sees to it that no one goes hungry. Children who
have left our kindergarten and started to school elsewhere come to the center in the afternoon after their
classes have ended. The children will range from
six to ten years of age, some older.

Some of the older girls enroll for domestic
science classes, some for sewing classes, some
for handicraft, some for dancing class. In the kitch-
en you can see thirty or forty little girls gathered
along the clean, oilcloth covered tables, or over
the white enameled stoves, mixing and stirring and
cooking and baking. In another room girls are sewing
or spinning or weaving baskets. They are seated in
a circle and their tongues are as busy with merry
chatter as their fingers are with the intricate needling
of the design. Elsewhere the older girls are being
trained in modern methods of housekeeping.

Now and then a visitor will come to see us. The
children always rise immediately as soon as a visitor
makes a call. After a brief but pleasant "Good afternoon, Mrs. Doe," they become absorbed in their

136   tasks again. I recall how this example of good manners greatly impressed Mrs. James Claire who taught our very first knitting classes and Mrs. George Douaire who shared her marvelous needlework secrets with our first class of incipient modistes.

When the dresses, embroideries, handiwork, and other items are completed, there is a public exhibition of the products. The preparation of the exhibits is always done well in advance of the great day. The girls and boys draw pictures, design the invitations, make posters, and issue handbills through

Sewing class with Mary Meade, 1940.

Sewing class exhibit, 1937.

the mail and to their neighbors. The dear little ones are born advertisers and a good attendance is inevitable. The exhibition of the sewing, domestic science, handicraft, and dancing classes is held in early summer and coincides with the end of the regular winter routine. There are songs and Italian folk dances by the girls, flag drills, and refreshments. As we conduct ten sewing classes weekly, the output in finished products is considerable. We take great pains to see that patterns and material do not duplicate, that the material is of good quality, and that

Domestic science class, 1940.

the pattern itself is pretty. For this the center has to
thank our teachers and the visiting staff of patrons.

And here I must confess a secret! Many so-called
imported models to be seen in exclusive dress shops
are often worn by our girls and young ladies before
they become common in department stores. Some
volunteer may come from her exclusive modiste's,
and lo, the pattern! Our training in fine sewing is
such that many of our girls have been able to follow
it as a livelihood as they grow older.

We conduct two domestic science classes each
week which include simple baking and cookery and
the care and management of table service. Our girls
are taught bed making, window washing, scrubbing,
how to clean and care for floors, linoleum, rugs,
carpets, and curtains. They are given basic instruction in household furnishings. We teach them how to
recognize cabinet woods and finishes and period
styles.

One's first communion day has traditionally been
surrounded with all the glamour possible, and on
that account it has always especially appealed to our
Italian Americans. The solemnity with which the
Roman Catholic Church surrounds the first communion of her little ones is amply supplemented at
the center where most of the girls make their own
first communion dresses and choose and hem their
own veils. Days pass into weeks, and the universal
refrain, "Yes, Miss Mary or Miss Marie, my dress
is all finished." For weeks everyone moves as under
a cloud of anxious anticipation. Finally the day comes
and the dark cloud lifts and Marghareta appears with
a wrapt expression on her face. The good news travels
along Loomis Street like lightning. Mothers and
daughters throng into the center to behold Marghareta's
first communion gown, miraculously finished at last.
Hard days may come and fond hopes go fleeting, but
within Marghareta's hope chest will rest the beautiful
white satin dress treasured against the day of a little daughter's first communion.

I should like to digress here for another memory

picture. When the first communion procession moves
with its flickering candles down the span of Loomis
Street and brings something like heaven to the city
thoroughfare, there are two people for whom this
day in their daughter's life is to have profound re-
percussions. They stand among the onlookers.
There she comes, shy, modest, and more demure
than her sisters, looking lovelier and more magnificent, thank God and his mercies, than any.
Praise the Madonna for having the dress finished.
For surely the Madonna or the guardian angels
came in the night and worked on the dress themselves. There comes Marghareta preceded by the
Italian band playing "Santa Lucia." There she walks,
flanked by the vigorous Italian pipers and by the
staccato serenades of firecrackers. One of the men
standing alongside is the father of Marghareta. The
procession moves slowly. With an explosive explanation to his astonished wife, Marghareta's father
dashes toward the church. He is going to waylay
some visiting priest and go to confession. Mother
of God, it will be a great day for Marghareta. She
will make her first communion. And there will be
her father and mother among the exultant throng
that sweeps toward the altar rail after the children
have received. Who would miss kneeling where the
young angels knelt or adding their own holy communions to that of their children's?

What was it Father Siedenburg used to say? "I
tell you, these are good people!" Yes indeed. That
is why I love every one of them.

We now come to the story of Mario, Mario with
the face and profile of a Greek god, wearing his
custom-made clothes as one to the manor born.
Mario for whom a doting family long ago set the
pattern we tried so hard to correct. Which we did
correct until Mario moved away in his later teens,
dropped from the intramural club, and merged into
the fast and footloose life of the city. Even so, I
never despaired of Mario because of one little thing
no one else noticed except Mario and myself. I had

once put his name on the honor roll with the other boys and girls for punctuality and attendance at church and the settlement. That evening when I went to add another boy's name, I saw that Mario had erased his. No doubt he somehow felt unworthy of the honor and had refused to doublecross his conscience.

I saw him off and on as the years passed. Then one night, quite late, the office doorbell rang stridently, imperiously; and when I went downstairs from our living quarters to the door, there stood Mario. I sensed his mood of utter desperation and need and I was fascinated by the terrible beauty of his face.

"Mario! It's fine to see you again!"

"May I come in, Miss Mary? It's late, I know but I . . . I . . . ."

I let him in and drew the curtain. Marie Plamondon peeked disapprovingly down around the bend of the stairs and quietly went back up to our apartment. Mario sat in a chair, his well-tailored suit crumpled, his hat a restless merry-go-round in his hands, his face down, eyes on floor.

"I will get you a drink of water, Mario . . ."

"No, no, Miss Mary. . . . Don't leave me. . . . Please!"

I studied the outstretched hand. Only the thick veins betokened strong passions. I took his trembling hand, then both hands, as he seemed to be reaching out for protection or stability. By and by he quieted. I listened in fear as he told a sordid story.

There had been a gang in the neighborhood which used a deserted barn as a rendezvous and for months had enjoyed a charmed life of baffling the police while they raped defenseless girls and women. Their luck in escaping the law and their braggadocio was such as to make them the legendary daredevils of the near West Side. They enticed ever more and more unsuspecting young girls into their trap; and partly through envy, partly through fear, they secured the loyalty and membership of an expanding number of youth for their miserable gang. Finally their devices entrapped Mario. That very night a lifelong friend who was a member of the gang had Mario entrapped. The stage was set at the abandoned barn. The lifelong friend had promised Mario a spicy night's entertainment, the crowning adventure of his life. Easily led and yet perplexed, Mario found himself in the gang's car riding toward the rendezvous.

But as the auto purred along Loomis Street, some familiar buildings appeared to Mario. The first days in the kindergarten at Madonna Center, the trials and troubles of a child's adjustment, the achievement of dependability, and above all the tenets of the faith rose before Mario and created a wall that held him from the imminent abyss. All the gentleness he had received at the hands of his mother, his sisters, and other good women, the innate courtesy he had showed them in return, the monstrously vicious aspect of the promised night's adventure sickened him so that, combined with the shame he felt when he considered his own decent home, he refused to ride on. The other occupants of the auto expostulated, even tried to force Mario to go along. But he leaped from the car.

Now he was here with me, a sort of unwilling father confessor pinching myself and asking if such things could be. I was glad that there would not be on Mario's conscience that most awful thing, a woman's cry of fright in the night; unless, as was part of the gang's pattern, she were gagged into silence, if not insensibility. I told the shuddering Mario that I thought he should go home, and I agreed to walk there with him. But I was not prepared for his frightened, "No, no, Miss Mary. Let me stay here. I'm as bad as the gang. I . . . I've been waiting for this night. I can't trust myself anymore!"

I knew he could not stay there in the office and it seemed that Marie had anticipated my dilemma; for presently the doorbell rang and there like manna from heaven stood our athletic director, Frank Mentone. Frank had an apartment over the gymnasium. Mario would thus not be far away, and I could see him again in the morning and plan some further

strategy. Frank told Marie and me afterwards that
he never spent such a night of physical and mental
distress in his life. A hundred times Mario begged
Frank not to let him go out into the night; and a
hundred times, like a drug addict, he went berserk
and fought to get past Frank and the bolted doors.
At dawn the struggle was over and Mario slept. After
breakfast Frank drove him home to find the youth's
family quite pleased that Mario had chosen to stay
with us after visiting with us late the night before.

Unlike many sordid gang developments this true
story had a happy ending for Mario. The deserted
barn had served as a safe rendezvous once too often
for the gang of rapists. The very night Mario would
have been there it was raided by the police and the
cowardly human beasts would never ravish a woman's
body there again. His "friend" sought to incriminate
Mario. But Mario had a perfect alibi. His narrow
escape brought Mario up short in his selfishness
and helped him to measure up to his better self. All
of those who knew what had happened were glad it
was Madonna Center which had halted him and that
the light we had tried in other years to hand on to
Mario did not fail.

Boy Scouts and Girl Scouts

As early as 1916 we had two Boy Scout troops active-
ly organized at the center. A chapter of the Boy Scouts
of America was established at the center prior to
1916, but for lack of funds and uniforms it merely
existed. However in that year mother, Marie
Plamondon, Catherine Jordan, and I met with our
Boy Scout leaders, Henry Littleton and Robert Ward,
to place our Boy Scout troops on a going basis. Henry
Littleton and Robert Ward are two Amberg grandsons.
At that time we had no accommodations of our own;
and the troop, such as it was, met two evenings a
week in the gymnasium of the Goodrich School near
the social center.

Boy Scout work is a lifesaver for the city lad, par-

ticularly if he is underprivileged. In asking our
friends to sponsor the Boy Scout activities we hoped
to make worthwhile citizens out of many an underprivileged boy; we were selling civic insurance to
keep boys out of jail and worse.

A Boy Scout camp is one of the finest places to
teach a boy the game of life, how to meet difficulties
chin up instead of taking the easy way out. I remember the first time we took the Boy Scout troop from
the center to Mount Pleasant Villa in Leland, Illinois.
It was a sunny morning in May after early Mass.
The haw trees and crabapples were in bloom, the
air was filled with the scent of the good earth, and
it made one promise to see that there would be
more such journeys into the countryside.

The complete change of environment from the
dirty streets and the influence of fine counselors
did wonders for the boys on the Mount Pleasant journeys. They learned to play fair, they understood the
comfort a hungry mind could take in a good book,
they realized the advantages which came from adherence to the finer things of life. They learned to
live cleanly, they enjoyed wholesome meals regularly, they improved morally as well as physically
and returned home after two weeks with the determination to profit by the experiences they had enjoyed.
It cost us seven dollars a week to keep one of our
boys in camp; the money was drawn from the funds
of the center.

When my coresidents and I were younger, we
often went with mother to enjoy a weekend with our
Boy Scouts. It would be hot in the city. I insist that
our slum children are the sensitive ones, the ones
who will step over a busy ant lest they crush out
its tiny life, who will stand transfixed with joy at
the sight and sound of a wood bird, who see magic
cities in cloud forms, and who treasure each simple
daily event in the secret places of their hearts.

"Where there is a will there is a way." Somehow,
wanting uniforms, our two Boy Scout troops managed
to have them vicariously. They borrowed uniforms

from a neighboring settlement and participated grandly in the First Chicago Boy Scouts' Circus at the Inter-
national Amphitheatre in 1916. It was well attended;
ten thousand tickets had been sold. Our boys were
so proud and thrilled. For many it was the first time
in their lives they saw wild animals. The most envied
of them all, Anthony Marine, enjoyed the thrill of
carrying hay and water to the elephants.

We suffered a temporary lapse in our Boy Scout
work at the center in 1921. My grandnephews,
Henry Littleton and Robert Ward, had taken on other
obligations and could be no longer with us. As late
as 1921, also, we were not able to equip our boys
with their own uniforms. However, what we lacked
in uniforms we more than made up for in hikes and
camping. The scouts explored Illinois trails and
played field games that cannot be played in the city
streets. They occasionally found Indian arrowheads
and now and then the remnant of a tomahawk. They
learned Indian lore around the campfire; and as
times grew better at the center, they actually lived
in a teepee. The Scouts learned to live and get along
with other boys, to begin, finish, and hold onto the
privilege of a camp task. They learned the practical
as well as spiritual value of being good instead of
being bad. They were being trained to be American.
Their health was looked after, too. And we saw to
it that they got all they wanted to eat.

Our Boy Scouts of 1934 were far luckier than those
of the earlier years, for by then we were able to acquire uniforms for them. Some of our Boy Scouts
took part in the Boy Scout Circus held at the Chicago
Stadium on Saturday, May 5, 1934. It was scarcely
believable what those in charge had done to capture
the illusion of the primitive outdoors within the four
walls of the great stadium. We were all very proud
of our boys and their leader, Frank Mentone. The
boys had outfitted and dressed themselves as Indians,
war paint, feathered headpieces and all. Each group
of the Boy Scouts went through the paces of "The
Great Plains War Dance" very much as they pleased.

It somehow achieved a harmony and poetry of motion that was delightful to us and made our boys very happy.

Participation in the circus made our Boy Scouts the envy of the neighborhood, for they paraded to and from the stadium with painted faces in full Indian war regalia, a sight no boy and few girls could withstand.

We were all very happy on June 29, 1937 when Frank Mentone was chosen to lead a delegation of Chicago Boy Scouts and their leaders to Washington, D.C., to take part in the National Boy Scout Jamboree. A vast space on the mall adjacent to the Washington

Madonna Center Boy Scouts with Frank Mentone, 1940.

Monument had been set aside for the twenty-five thousand scouts and their tents. They came from all parts of the United States, Canada, Mexico, and many other foreign countries. Our boys were anxious to give the best possible account of themselves. We had been at our wits' end for months to see that all our boys had new uniforms. And thanks to our many friends and well-wishers, they looked splendid. Most of the boys had earned almost every badge a scout is able to achieve. We were all so pleased at their appearances that we only halfheartedly denied the boys' pleadings to come along to Washington. But we were with the mothers, the fathers, and the families that went down to the depot to see the boys off with Frank Mentone.

Needless to say, the depot was bedlam. There were five different scout troops and five fife and drum corps. The whole neighborhood of Loomis Street was down at the depot with everyone speaking and laughing and crying at one and the same time.

After the train was gone, we began to watch the movies and newspapers for news of the Madonna Center troops and those other Chicago scouts Frank had in his charge.

Frank and the boys wrote back vivid letters. I find one in my scrapbook. It reads as follows:

National Boy Scout Jamboree
Washington, D.C.
July 2, 1937

Dear Miss Amberg and All at Madonna Center:

Assuredly this is the finest camping trip the boys or myself have ever had. Imagine twenty-five thousand boys in a large open-air arena, with no community practice or rehearsal, being able to sing scout songs and follow the leader with perfect timing. It was marvelous. I think even this one thing shows what wonderful training the Boy Scout program is.

Our crack Madonna Center patrol arrived in camp here near the Washington Monument at 8:30 a.m. Sunday, after our train halted for a while at historic Harpers Ferry. A fine old Virginia gentleman was on hand to tell us about John Brown and his significance in United States history and it was very interesting to learn our facts right on the spot.

Our past scouting experience came in very handy here. All we saw when we arrived at the arena was the base of the Washington Monument and a marshy plot of weeds, two hundred feet square, reserved for our troop. Headquarters gave us our tents and kitchen gear and told us to go ahead and make ourselves comfortable. Well, you should see those weeds disappear and behold your Madonna Center troop now. We won camp inspection three out of four days. There are fifty-one of us all told. We cook our own meals and serve ourselves from paper dishes which are then burned. No dish washing. Paradise, huh?

We went down the Potomac on a steamboat to visit Mount Vernon; and Luigi, whose father is a dentist, could not get over the sight of George Washington's false teeth setting right on that nice polished dining room table. The guide said the teeth were ivory and made by Paul Revere, but I tell you that Luigi thinks Mr. Revere will have to quit all his riding and spend a lot of time in a dental laboratory before he can make false teeth as good as his father does. Mr. Washington must have been terribly rich to have owned the fine mansion and buildings and all the land he had around here.

We have also been to see our Congressman, Mr. Long, and have passes for all the government buildings. I don't think we can visit them all, only I know that before we leave the boys will insist on seeing where Uncle Sam prints all his money. I sure want to thank you and Miss Marie for making this wonderful trip possible. Seeing even the dome of the capitol building for the first time, soaring over the whole city, did something to us that I will remember all my life. I hope that the work at good Madonna Center is going along in good style, because I sure am coming back with a lot of new ideas for boy work. We are praying for you both every night. I remain,

Frank Mentone
Scoutmaster

P.S. Sunday we went to St. Dominic's Church for
Mass. The priest came from the sacristy afterwards and met us in front of the church. He has
visited Chicago and knows all about Madonna
Center and has honored us by dropping in at our
campsite every day. F.

It was a great relief to welcome Frank and our
Boy Scouts back to Chicago. They were very glad to
get back; and though Frank and the boys were proud
of their record and trophy, quite a few were home-
sick.

Our Girl Scout work at Madonna Center material-
ized later than the Boy Scout work, but I often hoped
it could have begun earlier. A boy can rove to his
heart's content. A girl living in retarded surroundings has no such escape. Too often it was Florencia
and not Emilio who was sped to the corner saloon of
a Saturday night with the tin pail to be filled with beer.
While the girl naturally entered by the "Lady's Entrance," she was not always in the midst of ladylike
behavior. My coresident Marie Plamondon is by
training if not by nature an even-tempered individual.
But I have yet to see anything which would "set her
on her ear" like the sight of one of our girls "rushing
the growler" for her father and his thirsty friends.
There is nothing wrong with a glass of beer, and the
sociable Italian surely needed one on a hot summer's
night after the day's work was done. But Marie and I
felt that Florencia was not the proper party to convey
it from the bar spigot to the home circle.
We were, therefore, more than receptive to the
opportunities of the Girl Scout program. Marie
Plamondon took a leadership course at Girl Scout
headquarters to become familiar with scouting. In
1921 Madonna Center received a commission from
Cardinal Mundelein to organize the Girl Scout movement among the Italian Americans of Chicago's West
Side. It was logical that the organizing should be done
by Marie Plamondon. She had been devoting herself

to our girls, teaching them to sew and do housework, to make the most of their incomes, and how to give their children, when God sent them, the very best advantages possible. The Girl Scout work would amplify much of what Marie had been teaching our girls.

The cardinal's request coincided with the presence in Chicago of Gertrude Jackson, official organizer for the Girl Scout troops in Cook County. The conservative tradition, so far as girls' activities were concerned, was still prevalent among Catholics and others in 1921.

Madonna Center Girl Scouts, 1940.

Nevertheless, most of the mothers were in favor of the Girl Scout movement; and as a result of Gertrude Jackson's efforts and the cooperation of the pastors and mothers' clubs, troops were organized in many Chicago parishes during 1921.

There was a heavy mortality in troops and membership, however, and by 1923 there were only five troops flourishing in the parishes of St. Clement, St. Vincent, St. Sebastian, at St. Xavier College, and at Madonna Center.

150

I was very glad to have the Girl Scout troop at
Madonna Center because it reassured me that at last
my dear friend Marie Plamondon would be satisfied
with us, for scouting rounded out the whole scheme
of usefulness she had charted out for herself. Now
she could exercise her dear tyrannies and award
prizes and badges to the girls who excelled in cooking,
laundering, needlework, home economics, and the
like. Now she could take them to Mount Pleasant Villa
for the weekend. Now she could marshal her charges
into Holy Family for the eight o'clock Mass on the
official Girl Scout Communion Sunday. Now she could
depend upon little Felicitas to look as proud and well
costumed as high-toned Maria, since they were in
the same beautiful uniform.

Girl Scout work subsequently prospered at Madonna
Center, and later on much against my will, I, and not
Marie Plamondon was appointed director of the Chicago
Girl Scout organization. But it was Marie who bore the
heat and burden of the scouting day and weekend. And
it was Marie who saw that our Girl Scouts continued
to swell the congregation at Holy Family Church on
every Girl Scout Communion Sunday.

Dramatics

One main objective of a social settlement is to provide
wholesome leisure activities for children and youth
of all ages. We at Madonna Center have found that
dramatics is an excellent way of keeping a youngster
interested and busy.

Dramatics may be used as entertainment, pure and
simple, or as a means of character development. We
always consider it vital that as many children as possible have a part in any entertainment or play, even
if it entails an overlong program or creating supple-
mentary characters. We also strive to have dialog
which is worth memorizing.

It is always a pleasure to work with our children.
They are pretty and handsome, with eyes bright and
merry. They are instinctively simpatico, memorize

easily, and dramatize themselves into any part, however obscure or difficult. Since much of a child's best work is done when there is an audience, we encourage the mothers and children of other classes to drop in as spectators at rehearsals. Many times the children themselves create some new line or bit of stage business which is valuable because it appeals to a child's mind and is therefore incorporated in the playlet. This tends to make the dialog very spontaneous at times and the prompter behind the curtain is at wit's end to pick up the snarled thread of dialog so that the playlet may carry on. But this does not disturb the actors or the audience.

We naturally choose declamations, dialogs, and plays that are worthwhile, but not necessarily preachy. Amusement, clean and hearty, is the first essential. Plays with patriotic themes about Washington, Lincoln, and other great statesmen teach history in a very practical way.

Because of our limitations and because we can only draw upon the young person's leisure hours in preparing an entertainment, our drama instruction has to be more spontaneous than work in a schoolroom. In fact the young thespians' enthusiasm may quickly turn into rowdyism unless the drama director leads activities wisely.

I remember one December when the Sir Herbert Tree English Dramatic Company, then playing in Chicago, magnanimously offered their services for a pre-Christmas entertainment at the center. One of the skits was a broad burlesque upon drama of the "East Lynn" type. A long-curled, velvet-clad little Lord Fauntleroy met his older sister at the door as she literally blew in on the wings of a ferocious snowstorm of confetti, and rushed her toward the gouty figure sipping hot toddy at the great Tudor Gothic fireplace of the vast baronial hall, his boyish treble yelling at the same time in the best stage Oxonian: "Ow, fathah, see what our little Margie's brought from Lloundhon!" Literally for months afterward I would have to turn involuntarily at the sound of some unfamiliar voice behind me repeating the words in Loomis Street cockney. I may as well tell the whole of the plot, for the strange bundle little Margie carried in under her snow-laden shawl was no helpless babe, but a bottle of Scotch whiskey.

I reproduce here a typical program of a piano and dance recital such as is given annually by our children of eight to twelve years of age. I think the names of our little thespians are as beautiful as the music.

Piano   May McManus, Instructor

1 Betty's Flowers
       Antoinette Delsandro
2 Morning Glories
       Frank Delsandro
3 The Cello
   Peasant Dance
       Thomasina Minella
4 White Bunny
       Michelina Moraine
5 Camp Fire Girls
       Corinne Gentile
6 Dancing Daisy Fields
       Grace Tagliere
7 Spanish Troubadour
   Little General
       Elsie Batello
8 Elf and Fairy
       Carmelita Siracusa

Dances   Catherine Winn, Instructor

1 Opening Dance
       Dancing Group
2 Narcissus
       Marie Palumbo
3 Singing Games and Plays
       Play Class Group
4 Fairies
       Song and Dance Group

5 Sailor's Hornpipe
   The Barratta Twins
6 Spanish Dance
   Josephine Pintozzi
7 Country Doctor
   Dancing Group
8 Tarantella
   Dancing Group

Mary Synon, whose tale of early Chicago "The Good Red Bricks" has given her a place in American

Dancing class, 1940.

letters, was the narrator at our Easter entertainment in 1907. It was presented at the Marquette Council, Knights of Columbus and consisted of several tableaux, each of which represented a page of an illustrated magazine. Hence its title: "The Living Magazine." The funds were welcome, since after many years of no vocations at the center, one of our Cavallo boys had been called to the priesthood, and the proceeds were sent on for his support.

Locations for the playlets and plays depended upon facilities in the neighborhood until we were able to convert the former Bremner stable into a gymnasium, and as occasion demanded, into a theater. After 1922 we really began to make headway. What helped, of course, was that our wee actors of the dramatic and folk dancing classes had grown up and were now very mature and self-confident high school students, but they were still aching to try their feet on the Madonna Center boards. To encourage this and likewise give them yardsticks by which to measure their abilities, we often exchanged entertainment tickets with other settlements and with high school play groups.

In 1925 the Rosemary Club of Madonna Center presented "A Modern Cinderella." Aurora Lloyd directed the production, which was very successful. And Anne Pavese, editor of our center magazine "The Doings," played Cinderella delightfully.

Frontenac Hall serves the auditorium and entertainment needs of Blessed Sacrament Parish and was the scene of many of our more adult dramatic offerings I recall that after a couple of successful performances we were becoming so used to show business that our young people's acting was growing quite professional. This was especially marked when the Fidelis Club presented the gripping drama "Behind the Scenes" on May 29, 1938.

I should not like to leave a chapter like this without remarking that there was often intense drama simply in an Italian family's presence in America. Many a child who had been too speedily Americanized by "the gang" and who might have looked upon his parents as the "old man" or the "old woman" went home with a new vision after hearing little Marietta recite the actual experiences of her father and mother in their long journey to Chicago from Italy or Sicily. The old country took on a new importance, and parents gained in stature before their children as little by little the child teased the whole story out of them. Thus our elementary dramatics and personal recital brought a new appreciation of America as "the promised land."

And while our young people became more racially conscious, they also became more American-minded; for we never discussed Italian origins without paralleling our talk with a discussion of the effect of Italian culture upon America. Elocution exercises grew out of these discussions. They were often more energetic than grammatical. Prolonged applause greeted Tomasino one evening when with flashing eyes and eager lips he sped forth this impassioned credo of why he was glad to be an American:

Hey, you kids, I wallop the guy that says I am a Spik or a Wop. I am an American; this is America, with equal rights for all. This great country is so big and so new it has to be made up yet of people of different nationalities and religion, but the beautiful flag means equal rights for everybody; even for our folks just learning English at our night school. This American way is swell, kids. In school and on the playground no one says: "Move on, we don't like your face, or your race." Three strikes if they did. They're out. So obey the rules of the game, you guys, and let the best man win. I thank the country that sent my parents here. Hurrah for the United States!

Among our honored guests that particular evening was young Father Bakewell and two other Jesuit friends, Fathers Pernin and Breen. As we all sat listening to Tomasino, my Jesuit visitors told our Madonna Center staff that the attitudes expressed in the young people's speeches alone could justify the existence of Madonna Center as a place of Americanization.

During the Century of Progress Exposition in Chicago in 1933, Madonna Center cooperated with Chicago Commons, Eli Bates Settlement, Emerson House, Garibaldi Institute, and Onward Neighborhood social settlements in presenting an Italian program at the Children's Theater on the Enchanted Island. The Junior League Theater for Children also presented plays at the Children's Theater, and many of the offerings were on a very ambitious scale. But as I look back and reminisce, I do not think our own little actors or their efforts were overshadowed by the magnificence of the Junior League Theater productions. Our children were all amateurs, but singularly gifted ones. They were as cute as buttons and as bright as new dimes.

The end of the Federal Theater Project of the post-depression years was disaster for us as it was to many others who could not otherwise afford a visit to a legitimate theater. We were usually allotted blocks of tickets for our children. Though there are naturally divergent opinions as to the value of the Federal Theater Project, for my part I should have liked to see it continue.

Library and Publications

I do not think I should proceed without describing our library and what it meant to mother. The idea of the library coincided in mother's mind with that of the mission, each one complementing the other. She fully understood what good reading could mean in the life of an underprivileged girl or boy. As early as 1903 the library shelves contained several hundred volumes. Most of these were good novels of the period with mild detective stories of the Dick Merriwell variety, books of the Horatio Alger type, histories, subjects of general educational interest, and books of distinctly Catholic tone.

The library just grew like Topsy, because day in and day out mother begged friend and acquaintance alike to donate such library books as they could spare. Or, if they were only half-willing, mother would escort them to McClurg's or Brentano's and pick out the desired book herself, giving the donor the privilege of paying for it. Every now and then mother canvassed her acquaintances by mail seeking new acquisitions for the library. She had an understanding with the city librarian, Mr. Carl Rosen, to give Madonna Center any duplicate copies of worthwhile books the public library had no use for, and by that means she added many books to the library.

I well remember the day Mr. Rosen decided to pay a visit to our quarters on Newberry Street. What he saw of the library and its young patrons so astonished him that he cancelled the previous conversation he had with mother concerning worn and duplicate books. He offered then and there to install at Holy Guardian Angel Mission what amounted to a branch of the public library. I daresay that mother's refusal must have puzzled Mr. Rosen and made him feel that

Library at Madonna Center with Ed Scaccia, 1940.

mother was merely another woman who did not know her own mind. But the fact was that the mission activities were based primarily upon religion, and the library, small as it might be, owed its every book to mother's critical selection and deeply Christian nature. She would no more have surrendered the library to secular authorities to stock at random than she would have closed our doors and availed ourselves of the vastly greater advantages of any of the secular social settlements of Chicago.

Our library at Madonna Center is located in the same part of the former Bremner mansion where Marie Plamondon once detected the goats. Separating the literary sheep from the goats was one of the tasks mother performed so that the books would be instructive or entertaining and would in no way contaminate the minds of our young readers.

As our activities expanded we naturally sought to use the printed word as a means of acquainting our people and our friends with the work at Madonna Center. Now and then we started club papers which after two or three issues disappeared and passed away as vagrantly as clouds driven on by a summer wind. Some came and went because of overhead expense, some because of a scarcity of reportorial talent, and some because the editors who wrote the copy did not have the time or skill to process it. Except for the annual bulletins, which largely represent some printer friend's charity, we never until late years rose to the heights of a printed house publication like many other social settlements roundabout.

There were intermittent publications prior to World War I, many of them handwritten or typed for hectograph reproduction. In 1917 a kind friend donated an office mimeograph machine. It reproduced in quantity the letter which mother, Marie Plamondon, Catherine Jordan, and I used to write to our boys "over there." Its name was "Guardian Angel's Bulletin," and its format was a humble four-page, 8 1/2 x 11. In short, it was an amateur production; but what it lacked in sophistication it more than made up in love and thought and remembrance. So many of the boys had been writing back to us from over there that sending them the "Guardian Angel's Bulletin" was the best thing we could do.

Another mimeographed paper named "The Doings" made its bow in February 1925 with Charlotte Pavese as editor. You see, our former little ones were now quite grown up, feeling the urge of their talents to do something worthwhile. Then one of our discerning young men captured Charlotte, led her to the altar, and housekeeping soon removed a promising editor from our midst. "The Doings" then went into a tailspin, which was regrettable, as Charlotte was very talented and the mimeograph machine was capable of doing really good work in her hands.

In 1928 we began the "Madonna Centerite," which was to be a clearing house for all the news about our intramural clubs and groups. It was ushered in with fanfare to an enthusiastic--and free--subscription list. Each club or group had its own editor who was responsible for its own section of local news. The finished stencil was read by anyone of us who happened to be in the office at the time, Marie Plamondon, Catherine Jordan, or myself, and many artists of considerable promise undertook to relieve the horizontal monotony with vignettes and curlycues.

By 1930 the "Centerite" had survived the diaper stage and was now two years old, a most creditable publication which looked very attractive with its art work and colored pages. It even carried business card advertisements and was profitable for our friends and well-wishers in other parts of the city. But just as the "Centerite" reached its ultimate in typography and illustration, other activities called its editorial board, and one by one they quietly stole away.

At this writing we are quite without any house publication other than our annual bulletin. But I believe every social settlement should have its own publication, however humble. Though the years have not dealt kindly with our office mimeograph and more often than not it is covered with dust, I have a reverence for it. To me that little printing press of a sort has spelled out the running history of Madonna Center.

Intramural Clubs and Summer Programs

By 1907 the active members of our three sodalities for girls and young women were so numerous that they filled the church on holy communion Sundays. They were a significant part of the mission. By 1906 Father Dunne's original two groups of boys and young men had become well differentiated. One club was for lads under thirteen years of age, the other for youths of fourteen to twenty-two. Miss Hally had charge of the older group and Miss Doyle of the younger.

In June 1906 the boys gave a minstrel show in a neighborhood hall. They bought our baseball team some very handsome uniforms with the proceeds of the show. A feature of the minstrel show was "Yale Boys, '05," a scene written and staged by Raymond Binder assisted by thirty collegians from the various college fraternities in the city. Immediately afterward the garb of the young men of the neighborhood became very collegiate, airplane shoulders on the coats and peg-top trousers.

On the eve of Thanksgiving Day 1906 the boys gave an ice cream festival and realized a tidy sum to be expended on winter games.

In 1907 Mr. William Garvey took over the boy's sodality and built it into one of the most envied of all our groups. My father, Patrick H. O'Donnell, the noted criminal lawyer, and other well-known Chicagoans came to address the meetings.

On the eve of St. Patrick's Day 1916 we opened the Young Men's Club room. The members had refinished and repaired quite a bit of the donated furniture themselves. The program held selections by the Jesuit choristers from Holy Family Church, an address of welcome by Reverend J. B. Furay, S.J., the president of Loyola University, and a talk by Honorable Thomas F. Scully, judge of the county court. Vaudeville selections by James Yourell and Louis McMichaels followed the speeches.

Since the young men now had their own clubroom, they decided they were ready for a name. Father F. X. Breen of Holy Family Church was already director of our Holy Name Society and the young men had chosen him to be their spiritual director. Father

Frank suggested "Exempla Club" since it was the first and therefore could serve as an example and inspiration for the young men of the neighborhood. Having thus acquired a headquarters and a name, the Exempla Club gave its first annual dance at Emmet Memorial Hall on Thanksgiving eve 1916. The dance was a financial and a social success.

In the year the Exempla Club was organized, Father Breen, its spiritual director, decided to become its musical director as well; and he organized the Guardian Angel band. But Father Frank felt that life was too short to have to tolerate rehearsals, so he furnished the drums and brasses and recruited Charles Neuel, well known in Chicago musical circles, to be the director of the band. He was later succeeded by Professor Itso. Our band acquitted itself very creditably at the reception we gave to Reverend William H. Agnew, S.J., in July 1916 on the occasion of our friend's becoming president of Loyola University.

Alpha Mu Alpha Sorority was the high-sounding Greek-letter name of our young ladies sodality. It quickly became notable for its entertainments. Like the activities of the Exempla Club, Alpha Mu Alpha always paid its own way. Well do I recall the June "bouquet" when nine of our intramural clubs after paying hall rent, refreshment cost, and other miscellany of their dances, turned in a check of $213.00 to the mission office as a token of their appreciation.

None of the clubs meet without a director present. All the clubs have the use of the attractive kitchen on the second floor of the center. Thus in addition to other intramural activities there is a supper club composed of business girls who come to the center several nights a week and get their own dinner. All told, from five hundred to six hundred boys, girls, young women, and young men belong to our clubs.

When our children grow too old for the play groups, they are promoted into other activities. The boys join the Boy Scouts or one of the gymnasium groups. The girls join one of the sewing classes. Our high school

Working girls clubs with Catherine Jordan, 1940.

Frata Club with Frank Mentone, 1940.

students pass from the afternoon groups to our evening clubs. Our children are permitted to name their own clubs or groups. We have, for instance, the Regina, the Smart Set, the Rosemary, the Fidelis, and the Little Flower Club for the girls; the Frata and Nic-Con for the boys. The Nic-Con name grew out of the Boy Scouts' firsthand knowledge of Indian lore and means "Our Friend" in Indian language. The name was chosen to honor my dear father who was indefatigable in his attendance at club activities at the center. Our young people commemorated mother in the Agnes Ward Amberg Communion Guild.

I cannot close this section without mentioning that Frank Mentone, resident director in charge of our work among boys and young men at the center, is a typical Madonna Center product. He is a former Holy Guardian Angel Mission boy who first became a Boy Scout, then a patrol leader, then troop leader, and afterwards director of all our recreational activities for boys and young men. This includes Boy Scouts, our basketball, baseball, and football teams. Their many trophies proudly line the walls of my office. Mr. Mentone also coaches the girls' baseball team.

When vacation time comes for school children in a city of any size, parents naturally worry over what their children will be doing and how they can be kept occupied so as not to get into mischief. Worry is unnecessary for parents in our neighborhood, for in cooperation with the Board of Education we have developed a vacation school program which serves to take our children off the streets while keeping them amused and instructively occupied. Learning is a continuous process in the child; it takes place every conscious moment.

We try to make our vacation school a real contribution to the cultural life of the child. The usual school tempo slows down considerably and class subjects are those which will keep the child interested in spite of the heat and warm weather. While the center's classes in sewing, domestic science, dancing, and handicraft

Physical education class with Frank Mentone, 1940.

Madonna Center baseball team, 1940.

usually close after the June handicraft exhibition, storytelling and choral singing are subjects easily carried over into the vacation program.

The summer offers an excellent time for a child to become better acquainted with books. We form the different groups into reading clubs, and the teacher discusses each chapter with the class in order to draw out every child's impressions and develop his or her critical ability. The children are encouraged to read aloud and then to offer their classmates a digest of what they have read. Thus a child competes with himself; and when the checkup comes in autumn before school opens, he has moved toward the ability to give a recital or write a composition with a logical beginning, middle, and end.

Before I continue, I must pause to offer my thanks to the dear girls of the Catholic high schools who devote a great portion of their own vacation time to our children. In the early days of the center staffing our vacation school was quite a problem; but since organizations like CISCA have begun to work among the children in underprivileged areas, many of our earlier difficulties have been solved. As I write these memoirs an average of twenty-five girls from the Immaculata High School help with the vacation school and teach catechism classes at the center the year round. There are twenty-seven girls from Siena High School, one from Providence High School, and eight from the Academy of the Sacred Heart. Their work totals 481 catechetical hours a week and this time is dovetailed into the usual summer vacation school activities.

Our Catholic high school boys are also helpful, though not in the number and degree we or our children should like them to be. This is more than compensated for, however, by the increasing number of seminarians and young priests who in recent years have given their services to CISCA activities as moderators or spiritual directors of the vacation school classes, clubs, and play groups.

Story-telling time with volunteers from Siena High School.

I should like to reemphasize here the religious feeling we try to infuse into all our activities at Madonna Center. We strive to make this both explicit and implicit in all we do. Hence our desire for moderators and spiritual directors from among the seminarians and younger priests. No group activity meets without a simple but pertinent opening prayer. This is not a task but a pleasure. Ours is the singing strength of Catholicism, the true religion of joy. While we have mother church and dark nights of the soul to prove we live in a state of exile from our native land, it is only when we accept life's sunlight as well as its shadows that we arrive at the well-rounded Christian personality. And that, incidentally, is what we strive for in all those whom we serve and all those who serve with us.

Today we do not call our summer activities so much a vacation school as a summer program. The summer program remains fairly flexible in order to meet the needs of each day as it comes. Boys and girls under six years old meet from nine to noon, Monday, Tuesday, Wednesday, and Thursday. Girls seven to fifteen meet from nine to noon on Monday, Tuesday, Wednesday, and Friday for play groups, games, storytelling, paper work, story acting, handicraft, playground games, embroidery, flower making, folk dancing, and choral work. On Thursday mornings we schedule trips to the Field Museum, the Museum of Science and Industry, the Art Institute, and other interesting points. We have picnics for a different group each week in the park system or forest preserves. Swimming parties are held at the lake beaches. On Friday mornings we have library time with storytelling from nine to noon. Boys from seven to fifteen years of age also have a full program of activities, but because of their greater mobility, their summer program is neither as scheduled nor as standardized as that for the girls. Besides baseball, swimming, hiking, and handicraft, many of the activities are those devised for Boy Scout work.

Social Assistance Work

Miss Mack [Marguerite McMenamin] is our social worker at large; and with her competent group of helpers she keeps all outside matters of our neighborhood well in hand. But since the center is a clearing house for help and information, many inquiries come into the office. We strive to take care of these as best we can.

One true case concerns a godfather whose godson injured a woman while speeding in his car to a new job. The godson was arrested. He is now in jail. The Italians take the matter of being godfather or godmother very seriously. With the rest of the family the godfather has been trying to hire legal advice. They do not want the services of the public defender because they are too proud. Would the center please suggest the name of a good lawyer? We discuss the merits of several and finally decide upon one.

Next there is a legionnaire who tells us that a member of his post suffered a paralytic attack as a result of an embolism. There will be no immediate pension or other help for the sick man's wife and three small children. The American Red Cross serves such veterans and their families, but we undertake in the meantime to see what can be done.

Some of the requests seem topsy-turvy, as the wife who comes to the center with her ten-month-old baby. Both mother and child show traces of terrific whippings administered by the husband and father. She does not want to divorce him, but neither will she sue for separation. She only wishes our assistance in hiding from him for a few months "until he gets next to himself."

Then there is the mother of a certain ten-year-old named Michael. Michael has the face and form of an angel, but the fierce temper of a spoiled pet. The mother wonders whether we can find a place for Michael at St. Ann's Day Nursery for two or three months while she recuperates. Besides, she is having difficulty finding another flat since the landlord has

Miss Mack with neighborhood people at Madonna Center.

raised the rent. We have no room for ten-year-olds
at the nursery, and matters would end with the entire
staff having to take time off to recuperate, not only
Michael's mother. We counsel a good whipping as a
cure for Michael's tantrums, but we are doubtful
whether he will receive one.

Truly Christian is the sympathy our people have
for other people's problems. For instance, there is
the Italian mother who sat beside a confused-looking,
mere slip of a girl on a streetcar. Her discerning
eye saw immediately that the girl was pregnant. She
persuaded the girl to get off the streetcar and wait
at the corner drugstore until she came to the center
to voice her fear that the girl was in grievous trouble.
We hurry to the drugstore and bring her to the center
for comfort and advice. She very much needs advice
and care. Not only is she expecting a baby, but the
alleged father has disappeared. We immediately get

Children at Madonna Center

busy and find an understanding Catholic household that will give the girl shelter until. . . We do not judge or impute motives. In all such cases we have only one objective: the exercise of Christian charity.

In recent months birth and baptismal certificates have suddenly assumed mountainous importance. Those who were children at Madonna Center keep in touch with us as they grow up. We help them locate the birth or baptismal certificates necessary these days for defense employment. Since many unnaturalized Italian Americans technically became Axis aliens because of war legislation, we help the deserving over the rough spots of alien classification.

As already mentioned St. Ann's Day Nursery affords an answer to the problems of an employed mother with little ones to care for. We receive the children at the nursery in the morning, care for them, and have them clean and ready for the tired mothers in the evening. If the children are undernourished or the mother requires prolonged medical attention, we use our good offices to see to it that the children are placed in a good farm home where they will receive the physical, emotional, and other care they may be in need of.

We may be asked by a mother for advice concerning a miscreant father who neglected his offspring before he was sentenced to jail but after release wishes to return home. The wife does not want him, his five young sons do. We agree with all she has to say, but vote for the father's return. A home with a father is better than one without one, and the mere presence of the father in the house has psychological benefits for his offspring no substitute condition can possess. As part of such advice and adjustment, time is needed before an outsider can be sure of anything.

We are often consulted about the expenditure necessary for an adequate wedding or funeral. It used to be that an Italian-American marriage was often delayed until the family felt it had enough money for a grand wedding. This often left the families saddled with a heavy debt that had to be repaid for years after the marriage. We have gradually educated the guests to help share the expenses and thus ease the burden on the newlyweds. The wedding committee often calls upon us beforehand to discuss ways and means.

Another foolish practice we have helped to moderate is the grandiose funeral, out of all proportion to the family's finances. It was not uncommon for the bereaved family to have to sacrifice the entire inheritance and then some in order to have the most expensive casket and obsequies. We try to be on hand to fend off the ghouls who might take advantage of the family while it is in its first shock. Many a time we go from the center to the home of a neighbor and help with the last offices for the dying. We bring crucifix and candles, though even the poorest Italian-American family usually has these. We assist with the last physical offices, fold the toil-worn fingers over the rosary; and as the kindred and neighbors gather, we pray with them for the deceased.

These few items suggest the many services we render to our people day and night. I suppose that for the sake of the record it were better to be statistical. So many come to Madonna Center, so many difficulties are settled or smoothed, so many borderline cases are redirected to escape collisions with the police. But it would take more than social statistics to tell what we are at Madonna Center. It encompasses all the usual services of a social settlement. It takes in thousands upon thousands of children for catechetical instruction. It includes our influence upon fine young men and women who discover through the center that Catholicism expands rather than constricts their personality. It includes the continuing army of clerics and laity, young and old, for whom the center has been a magnet drawing them to Catholic action. It is a lodestone which draws the straggler back to the practice of the Catholic faith.

Yes, life at Madonna Center has its compensations. I would be doing scant justice to our laughter-loving people, however, if I permitted the assumption that they were all helpless. When things seem blackest, the comic spirit bursts forth to balance our worries with laughter.

I may as well remark that while I am away from the center it has been the custom for me to receive a daily journal of events from those in charge. They are typed by one of the secretaries and Marie Plamondon sees that the special delivery letter gets into the mail to reach me overnight. One night Marie had been very busy and mailing the letter became a later task than usual. As she went down the steps with the envelope in her hand, she found herself politely hailed by a well-dressed man at the wheel of a sleek new Packard parked along the curb. "Good evening, Miss Marie," the driver said politely. "Can I give you a lift, please?"

"Yes . . . and no," hesitated Marie. "I have a special delivery letter I must take to the mailbox."

"Take you straight to the main post office, Miss Marie!" he said. He stepped out of the roadster and was bowing Marie into the luxuriant upholstery when she recognized the autoist as a notorious neighborhood character with a prison record, a reputed strong man of the crime syndicate. What made matters worse was that it was past six o'clock on a summer evening and all along Loomis Street families had gathered outside on the front steps and benches for the cheerful conversation which marked the end of the day. Girls were skipping rope on the sidewalks, boys were playing catch in the alleys and along the curbs. "Hi, Miss Marie! 'Lo, Miss Marie!" heard my co-resident as she sank deeper and deeper into the luxuriant upholstery. But there was nothing she could do about it. She couldn't jump out, for the roadster leapt forward like a black leopard; and before she knew it she was outside the main post office. "Well," she said with considerable relief, "I'm here . . . and thanks very much for the ride, Mr. N----."

"Oh no, Miss Marie," announced her host from the depth of his wonderful gasoline charger. "I wouldn't hear of it. You just mail your letter, Miss Marie; I'll be waiting and I'll drive you back to the center."

I must also record an episode which for a time brought down around our ears much unwelcome notoriety. We generally encounter very little waywardness among our girls, but one time two teen-age misses had by their adventures and escapades literally set the neighborhood on its ears. Their parents were decent hard-working people. Court workers had called us in on the case, and we wanted to spare their families as much unpleasantness as possible. Therefore Miss Mack had them make regular probationary visits to the center. I think she hoped to learn the names of the youths who had led the girls into bad company. But while Miss Mack considered herself a good inquisitor, the wily two were more than a match for her. She found out nothing. On this particular Sunday evening, after wasting the better part of an hour fishing for information that refused to be forthcoming, Miss Mack finally gave up in disgust. "You two are bad, bad girls!" she excoriated. "Don't sit there giggling. Get out and go home . . . and know that God will punish you for your wickedness if I cannot." The girls hurried out much subdued after such a dismissal. When they reached home they found the parlor of their little flat filled with the usual Sunday visitors; and as they entered and slammed the door behind them, all the overhead plaster dislodged itself from the ceiling of the old structure and fell down on everyone's heads. To the frightened girls it seemed a direct visitation of heaven's wrath. No one was badly hurt. But the news of the occurrence and its circumstances leaked out and proved that Miss Mack possessed a power far more terrible than the evil eye.

I am glad to say the girls reformed. Indeed they became quite exemplary young women. And for a long time afterward Miss Mack's reputation in the neighborhood grew beyond her usual nickname of "Soap and Water."

Christmas and the Christ-Child Society

Christmas is one of the great holidays we eagerly look forward to each year at Madonna Center and our first really big celebration began in 1920. The Christmas tree is large and trimmed entirely with the handiwork of our children and young people. Tarlatan stockings filled with candy and useful gifts await each eager child. Madonna Center stands on a street corner and the crib is placed diagonally behind the two long front windows so that everyone can see the Bambino with the Virgin Mother and St. Joseph and the shepherds. Day by day the figurines are moved slightly. "The three wise men are on their way! See, they are not going back to their native land the way they came; they are going home a different way. Ha-ha, they will fool Herod. . . . Look, St. Joseph has put the Blessed Mother and the Bambino on his donkey and they are escaping into Egypt. Childish eyes can even see the pyramids in the distance." Creating the crib anew each year is a pleasant adventure. Children are formalists, no detail of the crib must be overlooked, no hit-or-miss rearrangement will be tolerated.

More than five hundred children join the festive singing of the beloved Christmas carols at the center, and there are many activities for grown-ups too. We welcome Christmas for its many blessings; stray sheep return to the fold, homes are restored, family circles are again completed under the mellow glow of the Christmas spirit. Christmas brings all sorts of visitors. Our crib is handsome in a material way as well as spiritually inspiring. The figurines are of wood and so superbly carved and colored that they rival the ones our people remember in Italy.

It is our custom to give every child a gift, however small. The gifts are distributed after the nine o'clock Mass on Christmas Day; and though many of the children have gone without breakfast in order to receive holy communion, they willingly stand in line to receive the little gift which seems so much in their childish eyes.

When father lived, he was always our Santa Claus. Considering the immense amount of chimney visiting Santa supposedly had been doing all the night before, he was always surprisingly active and cheerful. I knew that as he grew older father faced a herculean task as Santa. In the early days at Guardian Angel's the line of expectant children often reached outside the center, along the block, and around the corner. Yet father was reluctant to turn the gift-giving chore over to one of our younger male assistants. There he would stand by the Christmas tree, full of pride to be the object of such universal awe and curiosity. He was the traditional Santa Claus, artifically red faced, not too artifically white bearded, of considerable girth, and with the most benevolent smile imaginable.

The Christmas crib at Madonna Center, 1939.

There are usually two stacks of gifts at the left and right of the Madonna Center Christmas tree. Filling each gift package, giving each its distinctive Christmas appearance is a mighty task. Christmas economics require planning at least six months in advance. As December nears the gifts begin to arrive and are stored in every vacant bit of space. Organizing everything is a massive operation. Some volunteer workers open the bags and parcels. They carry the contents to the large table in the center of our work-room. Other volunteer workers sort, assemble, inspect, and wrap the packages. We use holiday wrapping paper and colored or gilt string for tying. The making of the Christmas gift cards which we enclose in each parcel is a mighty chore. I suppose we could save much time by having these printed, but always at the last minute we decide that printing is too impersonal. What it amounts to, finally, is that all of us at Madonna Center, older workers and younger, sit down and write, color, or paint the gift cards by hand. Mother was a beautiful penwoman and more than a fair artist, and busy as her days were she always managed to find time to make hand-painted gift cards that were much-prized and still are highly treasured keepsakes.

Christmas party for six hundred registered boys and girls of Madonna Center in the Notre Dame hall, 1939.

The Christ-Child Society is among the public heritages which mother left us. I would like to ask you to look in with me upon the tenement home of a mother and five children where every day is a desperate race for a few ragged clothes and bread and butter. The husband is in the prison for the criminally insane at Chester, Illinois, and will never return. To complicate matters there is a baby coming and there has not been the time or money to secure a cradle or one single item of the little wearables the infant will need. In the midst of the worry and desolation there is a knock at the door. A kindly messenger asks if Mrs. Doe lives here. The children assure him it is so, and he bestows upon the mother a plainly wrapped cardboard box, tips his cap, and departs. All the children cluster around the mother as with trembling hands she undoes the mysterious parcel. Within is an infant's layette, lacy, billowy, adorably dainty, complete to the last detail of white kid booties and a shiny rattle. There is no name and address of a well-off benefactor, no stab at the poverty of the poor mother, nothing but the heavenly lift of those four mysterious words that are written simply in one corner of the wrapping: "From the Christ Child." This is not only a corporal act of mercy; it is a symbol that God in his eternal vigilance has not forgotten and will not forget them in their hours of need.

The Christ-Child Society, of which my aunt, Mrs. Joseph W. Cremin, is president, was founded in 1877 in Washington, D.C. by Mary Merrick, an invalid. To recount the story of its thirty odd years of service and existence in Chicago is to recite the chronicle of a mustard seed that became a tree. It is a chronicle of tireless hands and a marvelous loyalty cementing directors and officers and coworkers and those who receive the gifts. Its membership includes, among many others, the names of hundreds of alumnae of the Madames of the Sacred Heart. It simply defies earthly logic to record how Miss Merrick, despite her cross of invalidism, began and carried on such a marvelous idea as the Christ-Child Society. Spreading out from Washington, D.C., each branch of the society is left free to develop its own technique of service. Here in Chicago my mother seized upon the idea of the Christ-Child Society as a way to help poor Italian-American mothers. I would like to insert here the words of Monsignor D. J. Riordan when he addressed the members of the Christ-Child Society of Chicago at their annual meeting in 1923:

Here in Chicago the spirit of that lovely woman, Miss Mary Merrick, took possession of one in particular, Mrs. Agnes Amberg, who during long years of her initiative, sound judgment, and zeal justified the trust placed in her by her associates. After being instrumental in the establishing of the Chicago branch of the Christ-Child Society, Mrs. Amberg held, by the unanimous insistence of her co-laborers, the post of president for twelve years until her death in November, 1919. I, who perhaps of all her friends knew her longest, knew her in the days of her girlhood when there was fore-shadowed in Agnes Ward the splendid qualities that in afteryears adorned the life of Mrs. William A. Amberg. I shall not say that others could not have done the work. But I shall confine myself to stating the fact that during all those years Mrs. Amberg, in spite of her other manifold commitments at home, in society, at the center, and elsewhere, also remained the very soul of the Christ-Child Society here and could not have been surpassed in the zeal and devotion to the cause she had espoused.

All of us at home used to wonder how mother had time for all these ventures, admirable as they were; yet she never neglected one iota of her manifold duties as a Christian wife and mother. Her administrative ability made her a veritable human dynamo and her faculty of surrounding herself with dependable assistants was, I think, one explanation of her progress and success in so many undertakings. She

Packing for the Christ-Child Society, basement of 1301 N. State Street, Chicago, around 1910. Mary Agnes Amberg, Mrs. William A. Amberg with granddaughter Mary Barbara Amberg (Pigott); Gilbert Ward Amberg with unidentified woman; and on floor, Agnes Zoe Amberg (Fiedler).

also seemed to possess a faculty of bilocation; she seemed to be everywhere she was needed at once. I believe the work of the Christ-Child Society appealed to her practical and mystical mind because it was both sensible and fairylike.

In many ways the Christ-Child Society supplemented activities mother had begun at the center. Additional centers were also established, like our own, for the instruction of Italian and other immigrant children. These centers were originated by mother in Chicago and conducted largely through the efforts of former pupils of the Madames of the Sacred Heart. But because of the appalling poverty of those they served and the expense of material and the effort that appeared to get nowhere, mother and her aides held joint counsel. The ultimate decision was to merge all the centers into one and confine the Christ-Child Society's efforts to outfitting the needy children of Chicago at Christmas time insofar as workers, material, and money made this possible.

This outfitting includes underwear, stockings, shoes, dress or suit, coat or sweater. Layettes are given to women with babies or to expectant mothers. Each layette box contains thirty-five separate articles for the wear and comfort of the baby, besides a gown for the mother. A holy picture of the nativity is also enclosed with Saint Luke's nativity story printed on the back of the picture.

At mother's death her special interest in the Christ-Child Society became the heritage of my sister Genevieve, Mrs. Joseph W. Cremin, who like mother and myself is an alumna of the Academy of the Sacred Heart. This was not with any wish for exclusiveness, but the alumnae of the Madames in Chicago have made the Christ-Child Society their special concern. Genevieve served as president of the Christ-Child Society for thirty years.

I do not know any other charitable activity which operates and is carried on quite like the Christ-Child Society. Not the least Christian aspect of it is the anonymous delivery of the gift box. As left at the door of the poor, the gift box bears only the four words: "From the Christ Child." The lack of publicity in the daily press, the unostentatious headquarters, the realization by the helpers that they are the hand-maidens of the Christ Child, all contribute to the happiness of the receiver and justify this extended mention of this admirable charity.

Mother's technique in conducting the Christ-Child Society's affairs was efficient and simple and it has been carried on by my sister and her helpers since our dear one went to her reward. Before the holidays mother would sound out father and then her friends with a view to finding some vacant assembling space for the receipt and packaging of the clothes and other things the members of the society had been preparing all year. The assembling space was preferably in

Genevieve Amberg Cremin (Mrs. Joseph W.) with her children, William A., Florence (Nichols) standing, and Noel (Perlitz) seated.

the Loop because of its central location. Of late years the Mayor's Clothing Fund has largely taken over the furnishing of clothing to poor children at Christmas-tide. But since "the poor ye have always with you," the contribution of the Christ-Child Society is still considerable.

For the benefit of the reader unfamiliar with the Christ-Child Society, I should like to summarize its work for a typical year. The assembling head-quarters are usually in a temporarily vacant floor of an office building. In all about ten thousand items of new clothing, suits, sweaters, dresses, shoes, underwear, snowsuits, blankets, mittens, stockings, and so on are given to nine hundred or a thousand children. Each gift box also contains a book, a toy, and candy for the little ones. Complete infant layettes containing all necessary wearing apparel and baby care items are distributed to poor mothers.

I never considered it a chore even when very young to accompany mother to the tea, which she and her friends of the Christ-Child Society gave for each other and their helpers in advance of the holiday distribution each year. I believe much of my own addiction to order at Madonna Center owes to the sight of the great space piled with new and neatly tied cardboard packages as uniformly and systematically arranged as if they had been assembled and cataloged by an army of efficiency experts. Every box had its key number signifying the age, size, and contents. To think of such parcels arranged with such care and wrapped with such expertness going out to the deserving was also marvelous. I know that mother and all those concerned with the work of the Christ-Child Society thought so too. They would leave the serving table with its cakes and tea things and be drawn to make a new survey of all the boxes filled with gifts and arranged in perfect order. All the old friends were there and many new ones. Father Morrison usually came down for an hour from his duties at the cathedral. If it was a fine day, we could even expect a visit from the archbishop. There was always a Jesuit Father or two, and perhaps Father Burke, Father Haney, or another of our good Paulist friends from Old St. Mary's. Everyone who was anyone to us was there, except the newspaper reporters.

I hope I shall not be considered too mystical or moving in the Celtic twilight, which is part of my heritage as my mother's daughter, if I declare that I believe that Christ still walks this earth to help those people he suffered so much to save. And if heaven is the abode of the unselfish, I know that much of mother's heaven is spent still heeding the cry of the earth's children and humbly going along with Mary and Saint Joseph and the Christ Child in further errands of his own.

The Depression of 1933 came riding through our midst
like some awful horseman of the Apocalypse, treading
down the little savings and hopes of the poor as well
as the fortunes of many who had been large-scale
bankers and manufacturers. Before 1933 relief work
on a three-meals-a-day basis had never been within
the province of a social settlement. After the first
stunning blows that called for all-out aid and assistance, we gravitated to the level at which we were
best able to operate. We supplemented the regular
relief agencies by serving in an advisory capacity
for our neighborhood. We also strove to keep on
hand a reserve of food and fuel in case of emergencies.
Not only food and fuel, but clothing, medicine, soap,
lamps, kerosene, and candles were kept on hand for
many of our people who had no place to go but to their
parish priest and Madonna Center.

We had to expand the services of our nutrition
clinic to teach the housewife how to use the food ra-
tions that now became available. We taught them how
to rotate the simple menus so that meals would not
become unappetizing. Our friends rallied to our aid
as best they could. Le Bal Tabarin held at the Hotel
Sherman in 1933 at $6.00 a plate brought in extraor-
dinary revenue. But expenditures for our people's
welfare were so insistent, the proceeds seemed to
slide through our fingers like fairy gifts fading away.

Our annual communion breakfasts, originally
designed as homecoming affairs, now furnished
vital material help as well. For though our young
people themselves were suffering, the intramural
clubs vied with each other to donate sustaining

purses that represented sacrifices far beyond each donor's slim resources.

With our national economic system well-nigh in collapse, an act of faith became the most insistent of our daily prayers. Until 1933 I never realized what a stern discipline an act of faith could be. Sometimes it seemed as though we could not go on another day, the demands were so great, the assistance so small.

I remember thinking how it might have been better had father lived, if we had his bottomless pockets, his sage advice to buoy us up and carry us on in the midst of the Depression's assault upon our self-satisfied American way of life. But as I look back upon those years, I have come to conclude that father could not have helped, could not have told me everything. A way of life with which all of us had long been familiar was ending, and we were too close to it to have more than a distorted perspective of it.

A heartening aspect of the disaster was the way in which those from whom it was taking a heavy toll kept their shoulders to the wheel for the good of their fellowmen. I recall how my valued young friend Edward L. Ryerson took on at great sacrifice to himself the duties of chairman of the Illinois Emergency Relief Commission. When he was forced by endangered health and prospects to resign the post, every business, civic, and welfare organization in the state felt duty-bound to tender him a farewell dinner of thanks.

In February 1933 we reached a milestone of recognition among our colleagues in social work, for on that date the regular meeting of the Chicago Federation of Settlements was held for the first time at Madonna Center. Making our kitchen facilities expand to cover luncheon for the distinguished visitors made us doubt our ability to match our performance to our hospitality, but fortunately our people turned out in full force and we all got along beautifully.

With the Century of Progress scheduled for 1933 and being heralded as Chicago's challenge to the pessimism of the Depression, all of us in social work knew that before the year was over we would be hosting colleagues from other cities. We strove to organize our forces so as to give as good an account of ourselves as possible.

Miss Mack directed Madonna Center's program for the exposition. Our day was June 6, 1933 in the Illinois Host Building. The program was to be under the auspices of the Chicago Federation of Settlements and the National Federation of Settlements.

The Century of Progress Exposition was well publicized. As the months passed we could gaze eastward and observe the gigantic steel frameworks growing along the lakeshore. One day there would be only a tracery against the eastern sky; and the next day there would be an immense structure sprawled over the landscape. Those of our children who had fathers or brothers working on the buildings had even more wonderful news. There was to be an Enchanted Island full of things to delight a child. There was going to be a real train that one could ride around the whole island for a nickel.

How to get not one nickel but hundreds of them for the Tomasinos and Fiorettas was our problem; and once again our friends came to the rescue. The Josef Urban Room at the Congress Hotel saw the first of a series of Celebrity Supper Dances planned to make the wonders of the exposition available to underprivileged children. The dances were quite successful, and twenty-four children's parties were scheduled for twenty-four different days at the lakefront.

While Madonna Center enjoyed its own day at the Century of Progress Exposition and while there were days for both the Boy Scouts and Girl Scouts, I would like to sidestep our own days and record the story of Children's Day, July 28, 1933. On that day two thousand orphans from Chicago institutions were admitted free. Other children needed only to pay a nickel to enter an enchanted realm of delight. Each party of

The Century of Progress Exposition, Chicago, 1933. Courtesy
Chicago Historical Society and Chicago Aerial Survey Co.

children was chaperoned by an official of the exposition. At nine-thirty our children were at the Fourteenth Street entrance to the exposition, everyone dressed in their very best, faces shining, eyes alight, every throbbing breast wearing its badge of identification, every little palm clutching its nickel. Madonna Center's delegation consisted of fifty boys and fifty girls and we had seven chaperons. These were little enough, for when we entered and our charges heard the beat of drums, the blare of bugles, and beheld the procession of children marching with them down the colorful Avenue of Flags, I thought that their spirits would jump right out of their tiny bodies.

Enchanted Island was opened to the children at ten-thirty. At eleven-thirty they went to the picnic grounds at the north end of the island for luncheon; and from that time until long after nightfall we rode, ran, or scrambled with our charges through the streets and byways of this modern Baghdad. Most of the concessions had reduced their rates to five cents for the day, but the rides on the Enchanted Island were free, and I believe each one of our children rode them all several times over. Our children marveled at the magnificent searchlights playing their colors into the dark sky and the play of light and color upon the mighty fountains. We finally counted noses at ten o'clock and found all of our children together, safe, and sound. We then convoyed our little ones across the great ramp that led toward the bus station. Not only had they indulged all the whimsies the exposition had to offer, they had visited the genuinely instructive exhibits as well, including the Italian pavilion.

They tell me that the Century of Progress Exhibition made its mark upon our midwestern culture and institutions. The perspective of the years is so close, I am not prepared to say. I find that my beauty-loving little charges were more awed by the Chalice of Antioch in the Hall of Religions than by the monster statues that guarded some of the great buildings, though the mechanical man, the glass woman, and the dinosaurs were close runners-up.

There was a special day set aside at the exposition
for a program by the Chicago Federation of Settlements and the National Federation of Settlements.
It was good to welcome dear friends and respected
colleagues in social service work, many of whom
we had not seen for many years. The general topic
for Social Settlement Day was "Broadening Horizons
in Community Work." While there were many prominent speakers, the principal one was Jane Addams
of Hull-House who spoke on "Settlement Work
Through Fifty Years." I do not think that remarkable
woman, long my valued friend, was ever in better
form.

In another chapter I pay my respects to her more
in detail. Though we had our natural differences,
all of us in social service work were intensely proud
of Jane Addams. For one thing, where I and many
like me had to depend upon personal stratagems and
pressured our society friends for needed support,
Jane Addams was the first social settlement worker
in our midst who was typogenic, if I may coin a word.
She was always good "copy," and the newspapers
realized it and gave her scads of space all over the
paper, whereas we were only able to secure space
in the society columns. She viewed social settlement
work as a necessary phase of the democratic process,
and she insisted that everyone whom democracy had
blessed should gladly contribute to a social settlement's
support. She welded together the old families and the
parvenues. She took conservative elements and gangster elements into a reform movement that swept all
before it. She made Hull-House a social oasis within
the heart of Chicago. Finally, she had the courage
to refuse tainted bequests.

Meek, unassuming wrens like myself were happy
to have a Jane Addams on the social settlement horizon. Madonna Center was a small settlement. We
trailed along in the wake of social reforms rather
than in their original planning. Miss Addams, however, had addressed state legislatures, had been
asked to Washington to address the Congress, had

been consulted about the social drift in the laws of the land, and she enjoyed the growing loyalty of young people. They were anxious to rally around her because she seemed to focus the social urges and the human magnanimity youth is so blessed to possess.

Jane Addams was the mistress of ceremonies of Settlement Day at the exposition, and I was glad it had been she who was called to make the oration of the day. She was the one among us most competent to take the listeners to the social hilltops and show them how the nation might reach the promised land of American democracy. She had little use for organized religion as such; yet she was essentially more Christian than many Pharisaic formalists. She believed her humanitarian principles to be individually come by; but a discerning critic could point out to her that without Christianity there would be no activating or lasting spirit to the democracy she continuously sought to implement through Hull-House.

Graham Taylor and Jane Addams, 1934-1935

Nineteen thirty-four was an anniversary year in social settlement history, the fortieth year of Chicago
Commons and its noble guiding spirit, Graham Taylor.
By 1934, also, much of the bickering of the early
days of social service had evaporated. The line between the religious and the secular social settlements
had become less sharply drawn. Graham Taylor of
Chicago Commons with his fine social sensitivity
was not simply the male counterpart of Jane Addams
of Hull-House. He was, like her, one of the pioneers.
His weekly column on social and civic topics made
the Saturday issue of the Chicago Daily News something to be looked forward to. In time his column
made itself felt even in the most ossified departments
of our city government and helped Chicago Commons
and all other social settlements achieve many of the
social and economic objectives for which they had
been conceived.

In my first years at Madonna Center we were
continually at war with some of the non-Catholic settlements. It was not their more prosperous finances
and accommodations which kept us spiritually in a
state of siege, but their proselytizing.

There were variations in our social viewpoints too
which puzzled me. Though Jane Addams was one of
the most truly Christlike individuals I have ever
known, religion as a Christian knows and practices
it never held meaning for her. Her life moved upon
a humanistic level motivated by social sympathy
and an urgent sense of the shortness of life.

I remember that when Ellen Gates Starr, co-
founder and coresident with Miss Addams at Hull-

Ellen Gates Starr

House, announced to her lifetime friend that she intended to become a Catholic, Jane received the
astounding news with less concern than if a member
of the Hull-House staff had gone Republican. And
yet Ellen Gates Starr had arrived within the Catholic
fold by a way which most intellectuals would find
impossible; namely, through seeing the impact their
faith made upon the simple lives of the Italian
Americans, Mexicans, Greeks, and other underprivileged people who flocked to Hull-House.

To Jane Addams, schooled as she was under
sophisticated non-Catholic teachers, certain mis-
conceptions of the Catholic Church were natural. To
her medievalism was synonymous with feudalism and
serfdom, and she could not possibly imagine serfdom

was simply a phase of industrial and social transition. The apparent incompatibility of liberty and authority in the Catholic Church likewise presented Jane Addams with many insurmountable difficulties. I do not over-look the effect upon Miss Addams of the morals of some Catholic politicians and civic figures with whom she had to fight for the rights of her charges. It was a thesis of Jane Addams that a social policy was also a population policy. Limiting a family in order to ex-pand its economic status was inherent in all the social objectives of Hull-House. As a result birth control clinics were added to its program.

Graham Taylor differed from Jane Addams on the population-economics question. To him the Catholic attitude on birth control appeared logical. He had a deep understanding of religion and the in-dividual's and society's need of it. He agreed that the Catholic Church was the most universal, the most adaptable, the one most socially disciplined and beneficent. He could not bring himself to mem-bership, but often agreed with us that if any religion held the germ of survival in a more or less sick world, it would be the Catholic. Knowing Mr. Taylor and his opinions as we did, we often prayed that he might receive the gift of faith. However, this was not to be--and who were we to judge? We trusted each other and were never in doubt of our true sentiments toward each other. Therefore it is pleasant to find the following letter among my treasured keepsakes.

Chicago Commons
955 West Grand Avenue
Chicago, Illinois

Miss Mary Amberg and Miss Marie Plamondon
Dear Comrades in Settlement Service:

The beautiful yellow roses coming from Madonna Center to Chicago Commons during its Fortieth Anniversary Week drew our hearts in both groups more closely together than ever.

Graham Taylor

Through not a few of these later years has our fellowship heartened us both in one and the same spirit with which we love to work with and for our needy and responsive neighbors.

Please assure all at work with you in contributing personal service or financial support how highly we at Chicago Commons appreciate the cooperation of Madonna Center in its work for the Greater Chicago, and how we cherish and reciprocate the fellowship of its resident workers.

Grateful for your cooperation in our anniversary.

Cordially yours,
Graham Taylor

On May 21, 1935 our preparations for the crowning of the Blessed Virgin were under way when we learned that Jane Addams, our colleague in social service and head resident of Hull-House, had gone to her reward. I visited Hull-House to pay my respects to its dead resident. The quadrangle was a veritable bower of flowers. They filled the ground space and overflowed from the windowsills and the balconies. Knowing Jane Addams as I did, I could scarcely imagine that vital, bright spirit was dead and gone from the place and the people she loved. I could imagine her darting about in the nervous way she had, pleading "Why are you making such a fuss over me? I'm not dead!" The same thought remained with me when Ellen Gates Starr, Marie Plamondon, and I attended a fellowship meeting, a memorial to Jane Addams at Chicago Commons on June 4, some days after her burial. I remember speaking with Marie about having one of the Jesuit Fathers say a requiem Mass for Miss Addams. Ellen Gates Starr seemed to have solved matters. "O, that's all right, my dears," she put in quickly. "I shouldn't trouble. I had a Mass said for her soul this morning. I thought it would do her more good than our just sitting here praising her."

In God's inscrutable design the household of man needs its Marys and its Marthas. Since her death, now many years past, I still feel there never was and never will be another in social work quite like Jane Addams. To us shy wrens of social settlement work the advent of a personality like Jane Addams among us was almost Pentecostal. We all took fire from her bravery, her determination, her insistence that her work was one of the most important in America. She was absolutely without side. She would be up and about and have hours of work dispatched while the average woman was still about her toilette. She was casual about her apparel, and yet I do not recall another woman who always seemed so well dressed, so neat, so clean. No wonder that with her passing one chief prop of Chicago social settlement

Jane Addams

life seemed gone. I am sure that St. Peter whom she
strangely resembled must have discerned a fellow
spirit when Jane arrived at the heavenly gate. With
her own hand she had not only fed the hungry, clothed
the naked, visited the imprisoned, and comforted the
sorrowing; she had made many of those about her go
and do likewise.

Though Jane Addams used the most modern social
tools and materials, she had developed at Hull-House
a variation of an age-old humanitarian agency, the
Christian hospice. One other fact I do not believe
has ever been sufficiently stressed by her biographers
is that while she held fast to the ideals by which she
lived, Jane Addams never taught the ethics of social
responsibility without being willing to pay its price.

Thus at a time when Hull-House was in dire financial straits she flatly refused a bequest of many thousands of dollars left to Hull-House by a donor whose method of securing his wealth she could not condone. She played no sides and nurtured no special favoritisms. She was forcing aldermen to vote for slum clearance in her neighborhood at the same time she was warning congressmen to vote racial equality for northern and southern Negroes.

Race prejudice was totally foreign to Jane Addams, as it must be to all social workers. We know now that our treatment of the Negro has been both un-Christian and uneconomic. In this attitude as in many others Miss Addams was ever in the mainstream of American social thinking. She had a social spirit so large and universal-minded it was essentially Catholic.

Summing up, I think that we owe inexpressibly much to Jane Addams for helping through Hull-House to bring a new dynamic into the pattern of city, state, and national life. To the last she never lost a child-like capacity for wonder which those who did not know her very well could not quite comprehend. In her dealings with politicians and statesmen she relentlessly pursued her course of action.

In a chronicle of this nature a chapter of obituaries is inevitable.

I recall that seventeenth day of October 1929 when I received the news that Bishop Dunne had passed to his eternal reward at the age of sixty-five. He had left Guardian Angel Parish in 1905 to become chancellor of the archdiocese of Chicago, and in 1908 he was consecrated bishop of Peoria. It was hard to believe that our former spiritual director and co-worker at Holy Guardian Angel Mission could have died so soon. He was not only a good priest and chief pastor, he was also charitable, magnanimous, and intellectually alive. We had lost a lifetime friend and adviser.

Our older people were likewise crushed by the news. Most all of them could look back over the years to the cheery young priest who saw not the outer garb of poverty, the outlandish clothes, the soiled hands and dog-eared shoes, but the pristine goodness of each meek and humble body bearing within it as in a temple the Holy Spirit. More important, perhaps, he had been for our Italian-American immigrants a typical American, an antidote to those who derided the potentialities of the faith which was our people's birthright. He had set up before them, young men and young women, boys and girls, the reality of a two-fisted Galahad, a hardy fighter and coworker of Christ, a man who could lay aside his gentle expostulations and don a pair of boxing gloves to help some brassy contender find his place. May he rest in peace!

Rt. Rev. Edmund M. Dunne, D.D.

Some years later, on March 24, 1936, death took another of our loyal coworkers and friends, William J. Bogan, Chicago's superintendent of schools. Madonna Center owes much of its social and educational stature to him.

Mr. Bogan was born on Mackinac Island in 1870. Following early teaching in Michigan he came to Chicago and taught at the Washburn Elementary School for seven years while completing graduate and post-graduate degrees in education at the University of Chicago and Armour Institute. From 1900 to 1904 he was principal of the Washington Elementary School at Grand and Morgan Streets. When school board officials were seeking a capable head for the new Lane Technical High School in 1905, they found him in Mr.

Bogan. His work at Lane was so satisfactory that he remained principal there for nineteen years until 1924. In that year he was named assistant superintendent of schools under William McAndrew. In 1928 the school board unanimously elected Mr. Bogan superintendent of schools, which post he held until his death in 1936.

While assistant superintendent of schools and later on as superintendent, he came to Madonna Center to teach catechism classes in his free time and gave generously of his vast store of pedagogical experience. Had it been up to Mr. Bogan, we could have had an adult education program long ago in the Dante School.

When he became superintendent of schools we saw less and less of Mr. Bogan, though he continued to aid us by every other means possible. There was a question, false as its base might be, which challenged the propriety of a public school official giving so much of his time to a purely religious social venture like Madonna Center. The truth is that Catholic tax money helps support the public schools. As Catholics we have no quarrel with education; but life is made up of differences, variety gives value, and if one is ever to enjoy democracy it must be where the lion can lie down with the lamb. The nation needs our parish school ideology and we can benefit by public school assistance.

Our dear friend and adviser Father Frederic Siedenburg died on the twentieth of February 1939. He was a sociologist and priest who gave his utmost to Madonna Center through the years. Without waiting for some future chronicler to give Father Siedenburg his biographical due, I shall very briefly review his career here.

Father Siedenburg was the son of a Lutheran father and a Catholic mother. He received his early education in the public schools where in addition to being an excellent scholar he was very good at baseball. He remained an ardent baseball fan all his life. By reason of his far-flung Jesuit correspondents, he was an outstanding philatelist; and when he had to give up collecting, he managed to dispose of his stamps at a hard bargain. He also founded the Illinois Catholic Historical Society in which my father, William A. Amberg, was so interested.

In 1924 Father Siedenburg was one of the American delegates to a congress of sociologists held in Germany that year. Afterwards he toured Soviet Russia, and he told me that on his first morning on Russian soil he offered Mass for "Holy Russia." He felt that for its own good Russia must in time return to that faith which alone could fully ennoble and round out its economic and national destiny.

Father Siedenburg could speak and write of the Russian revolution as an eyewitness, and later on when he returned to Chicago he urged the deportation of all communists and un-American deluders. Yet as a priest and pastor of souls atuned to spiritual forces, he was impressed as well as troubled by the social dynamic of Soviet Russia.

The school of sociology which Father Siedenburg established at Loyola University here in Chicago was the first of its kind in any Catholic university in the United States. He can be acclaimed as the first clerical scholar in the field of social psychology in America. It is due to him that sociology has become an established phase of Catholic action.

Like all scholarly Jesuits, Father Siedenburg was a frequent contributor to religious and sociological journals. Together with Jane Addams and Graham Taylor he formed the first motion picture censorship board in Chicago.

Before he left Chicago in 1932 to become executive dean of the University of Detroit, Father Siedenburg had been a member of the State Welfare Board of Illinois, president of the Illinois State Conference on Public Welfare, and chairman of the Chicago chapter of Professional Social Workers.

Though always spiritually a sociologist-priest, when appointed to the University of Detroit, Father immediately proceeded to help Father John P. McNichols realize his dream of a college of dentistry.

Rev. Frederic Siedenburg, S.J.

After being in his Detroit post scarcely two years, he was appointed by President Roosevelt in 1934 to the Detroit Regional Relations Board designed for the settlement of labor disputes in that area. Father was an all-out supporter of President Roosevelt's social and political beliefs.

Father Siedenburg was also invaluable as a priest, and I remember in the midst of his manifold duties he came down to our mission to hear confessions of a Saturday afternoon and evening. It was around Easter time and we felt it only right that we should warn him that he might have some hard cases. Afterward he stormed into the office. "What did you mean by hard cases, you Pharisees?" he asked not too gently. "I tell you, they are good people . . . good people."

He loved the Negro with a Christlike understanding I wish more of my fellow Catholics possessed. If God has indeed any chosen people nowadays, I am sure in Father Siedenburg's mind it was the Negro race, especially in the United States. While he rebelled at the social reasons for their humble condition and lowliness, he loved them all the more because of it.

I remember how one night Marie Plamondon, Father Siedenburg, and I were returning from some meeting or other, and the State Street car upon which we rode was filled with Negroes going home from work. There was one particular one, quite an old Negro, rather soiled with shovel and patched overalls, whose thick kindly lips laboriously followed the words of a dog-eared Testament he held in his hands. "I guess you and I belong together, sir," remarked Father Siedenburg as he moved in beside him and took out his breviary. And that was the way they sat and read until the three of us changed cars at Roosevelt Road. I have always believed that Christ still walks this earth; and somehow that night in the crowded streetcar he seemed very near.

It occurs to me now that in this last chapter I should like to sum up many of the intimate talks I have had with young and old who wish to make a career of social work.

I should not wish the neophyte in social work to gather from my Job-like plaints in previous chapters that the greatest need of a social settlement is money for its ever-needy budget. Everyone engaged in social work knows there are dark nights of the soul. The scantily financed social worker who follows his or her calling has found that with the low budget there are the ever-present little lightnings of the merciful Christ. There is no substitute for the kind word of encouragement spoken from an understanding heart. Even if one encounters a poor derelict who has no place to go, we can remember that the Son of Man also had nowhere to rest his head. There always remains the innate dignity of the human being; there always remains faith, hope, and charity; and the greatest of these in the social worker's vocabulary is charity. Even when we feel we have been imposed upon, it is not wise to assess guilt without reference to a person's situation. We must consider their poverty before we pass judgment. When a policeman or a property owner or a judge tried to tell me how hopelessly bad one of our Tonys was, I would insist that they consider Tony not as an individual but as a typical specimen of an underprivileged class. If that is done, any social worker will find to his or her surprise that bad is a very relative term.

An unlimited capacity for decent pity is vital to the social worker. I well recall a neighborhood character

named Two Gun Charlie. He was a brigand, a hijacker
of liquor trucks in the prohibition era. He was rumored to have and indeed looked as if he might have
had several notches on his revolver. Yet one never
saw him meet a child on the street without giving
the little one candy from his bottomless pocket.
Marie Plamondon thought such a gentle soul could not
be as bad as gossip related. It had been whispered
about that Two Gun Charlie's days were numbered
and any day now we might expect word of the assassin's shot. Marie gained his confidence, taught him
how to say the Act of Contrition, and insisted that
in an emergency he must not forget it. After much
persuasion she even secured his consent to meet her
on a certain Saturday afternoon when she would accompany him to church and assist him in preparing
for confession. But that Saturday as Marie went toward
the street corner rendezvous, guns barked hard by
and a black sedan screeched past in a cloud of dust.
A familiar form lay crumpled on the pavement. Two
Gun Charlie was beyond entering any church by the
power of his own two legs. He was quite finished with
life; he knew that. But as the curious quickly gathered,
he awaited Marie forgetting his physical agony as he
weakly murmured the Act of Contrition. His eyes
lighted up when he saw her. He told her with almost
his last breath that he knew she would come. Something intervened, but he couldn't disappoint a nice
lady who had hoped for his reform and who was willing to believe a little prayer could get even a poor
devil like Two Gun Charlie into Christ's kingdom.

This is an extreme case. But it shows how the
Catholic social worker can offer Christian aid and
comfort to the needy. Men and women with genuinely
magnanimous natures, deep sympathies, and disciplined Christian outlook are vitally needed in social
settlement work. We need the type of worker who
keeps his or her feet on the ground, who is not fear-
ful of mistakes and discouragement, who has an
abiding faith in the ultimate goodness and dignity of
human nature. Finally, the Catholic, or any Christian

social settlement, needs workers whose good deeds are not done in the hope of gratitude but because they are what the other deserves. Madonna Center has seen many such beautiful flowers of Christian faith. They have made our grounds and quarters as beautiful as the setting and structure of some vast and beautiful cathedral, a magnet which ever draws to us young hearts and adult souls.

I must not allow myself to forget that this is a chapter of ways and means as well as encouragement for the young or older person who feels a vocation for settlement work. It will be a mistake if any who wish to help people along the avenues of social endeavor wait for a full set of helpful circumstances or hope for a divine imperative to light them into a social career. No confessor or mistress of novices requires a one hundred percent visualization of a vocation to allow someone to enter the priesthood or the religious life. Nor is such a vision necessary for the social worker. When Christ at the last judgment passes the verdict on those who come before him, it will depend wholly on their responses to others' needs. It will not be based upon whether one had a Saul-and-Damascus sort of call to social work. He will simply assess and reward us on our basic duties as Christians. My suggestion for the novice in social work is to go forward with a good heart and a good will, assured that the virtue of magnanimity will be theirs. I must add, however, that life has a way of adding more duties and more burdens upon such good spirits whose social vision often outstrips the poor mechanics by which their vision is to be realized.

Social settlement workers must ever pray and plan for their daily bread. While Madonna Center is recognized in the Community Chest allocation, while our workers through the tag days for children's social agencies secure some funds for St. Ann's Day Nursery, we have come to depend upon the proceeds from our annual post-Easter charity dance. It is our financial index for the year.

Anniversaries and jubilee celebrations also are occasions when there is an encouraging inflow of financial aid. I can never feel grateful enough to our many friends for the financial bouquet they garnered for our fortieth birthday. Our annual report to friends and benefactors suddenly swelled miraculously. Page after page of advertisements from individuals and friends dismayed us, for we realized these would never be read by sufficient of the public to pay for the advertising space. But as a going record of boundless appreciation and a wish to be of aid, our fortieth anniversary report will long remain a milestone in our history and an inspiration to all of us. Happy the social settlement which at its fifth or its fortieth anniversary can have made itself so much a part of the fabric of its town or city that it can invite such a bouquet, not alone from the people it serves, but from the entire community.

No matter how the war continues or ends in the Far East, the vast mission fields built with such an enormous price of great souls and vast financial expenditure may be lost to us for decades if not for centuries. We Catholics now need to take stock in our mission fields at home. If this is to be the Mystical Body's newly woven crown of thorns, let us bow to it and survey the vast religious and social potential of our mission fields at home. We must more than ever bring souls to Christ.

We must resolutely set our face and our strength against all "isms" that give the lie to Christian charity and forbearance. We must appraise all racial stocks at their best instead of their worst. We must fight the intrusion of Jim Crow techniques in the North and its extensions in the South and campaign for social and economic justice for our Negro brothers. To demean the integrity of a fellow human is self-damning; it cries to heaven for vengeance. We cannot permit demagogues to exploit the worker's prejudices in order to create riot conditions that will encourage despots to crack down upon labor's natural rights. We cannot as Catholics indulge any kind of

Mary Amberg and her nephew, Lt. William A. Cremin, 1942.

anti-Semitism without suffering our spiritual and moral stature to go into a vast decline. We cannot as Catholics be blind to any social implication in our Christian doctrine and our faith. For the kingdom of heaven is seen through our works upon earth. In too many countries we see shattered the Christian principle that the human being is important as an individual, that far from being the leaven in the mass of his fellow humans, he is a mechanical unit of the state.

If our work at Madonna Center has never been as varied or as progressive or as well-financed as we might have wished it, it has still been more hopefully progressive for our people than any social ideology they might have been subjected to in their

own country. We of Madonna Center believe our settlement has made a good contribution to these troubled
decades of social defense and social offense.

This chronicle began in the month of May 1940. It
is being finished in October 1942, a month consecrated to the Madonna under the title Our Lady of the
Rosary. Our Lady's picture has always been the sacred ikon of Madonna Center. The week or so of sum-
mery October days which delude Chicagoans has gone.
The elms outside on Loomis Street have shed most of
their crisp brown leaves over the grass. We are back
in winter weather of sorts. Some of the boys have
gathered some empty crates from the alleys and a
fire is roaring in the grate. We are serving tea this
afternoon for matrons and patrons of the center.
Marie Plamondon is a one-person receiving line at
the door. She is the same lanky Marie, her vivid
gift of language mellowed somewhat, but still pleas-
antly acrid. Here at the center we are not cut away
from all kindred relationships. Here comes Dorothy
Plamondon and Virginia Amberg. Virginia is the third
generation of our family to come and be interested in
the work of Madonna Center. The women discuss
some pressing social or financial problem. Others
are busy with our prospectus for 1943. We are re-
viving our Red Cross unit and nearly every child and
teen-age member of Madonna Center has some part in
defense activities in our neighborhood. The Girl
Scouts and the Boy Scouts have refurbished and en-
larged their emergency service units; the intramural
clubs and various classes all live and move in a state
of intense rivalry over such salvage operations as
collecting newspapers, rubber, and scrap metal. In
fact there is an unsightly mass of the latter outside
our usually neat entrance.

Our visitors take it all in stride. They are not
panicky, though the return from the annual tea dance
this year was not as large as the year before. We
therefore take courage and hope from their insouciance.
Like them, we believe that the most patriotic contribution Madonna Center can make to the neighborhood,

the city, and the country at the present time is to maintain all our normal activities at their usual high level.

In Chicago there are fifty settlements like Madonna Center, neighborhood houses, youth organizations, and the like who have the same worries we do about today and tomorrow's daily bread for their people. Most of us, the dear Lord knows, have long ceased to consider ourselves a luxury for our people or the municipality.

We have always been busy at Madonna Center; and we and our visiting helpers know that henceforth we are going to be busier than ever. Yes, we must carry on. So again we take up the balance sheet of proceeds from the annual tea dance and the plans for its successor next year. There are several holes in the balance sheet that we must make an Act of Faith about and fill up somehow--as usual. I look at the picture of the Madonna over the mantle wondering to myself if we are not forever imposing upon her too much. After all she is in her deserved heaven on earth. Mary scrimped and saved and felt the pinch of poverty enough. But then it occurs to me that for Christ's sake and our redemption she became the Madonna. We have also made her Our Lady of Perpetual Help.

So one looks at the unelastic figures on the credit side of the balance sheet, and the very expansive ones on the debit side. I make a little prayer to my dear dead mother. I whisper to the Madonna my hope that Madonna Center will ever exist and that in it our people and our children will ever find inspiration and encouragement and understanding.

In her mystical yet matter-of-fact way mother sensed that to give was the essence of Christian living, and it is the essence of a Christian social settlement. I cannot think of a better way to end my chronicle than to repeat the verse which I recorded earlier. It is my rededication to my reader and my people, my credo of life.

What if thy need but adds unto my burden,
What if I stumble 'neath thy load -
  Still thou to me dost bear the Christlie guerdon,
  Thou art His angel on Life's road.

  Holy, holy, holy is thy need of me,
  Holy, holy, holy is my gift to thee.

Marie Plamondon, Cardinal Stritch, and Mary Amberg on the occasion of Mary and Marie's receiving Citations for Distinguished Service awarded by the Alumnae Association of the Sacred Heart at Barat College, November 21, 1950.

Mary Amberg with Children of Mary who were volunteer workers at Madonna Center, 1954. Standing: Mrs. Frederick Axley, Mrs. George Lane, Mrs. George Fiedler, Mrs. Harry Drake. Seated: Mrs. George Caspar, Mary Amberg, Mrs. George Douaire, Mrs. Richard Sunderland. In front: Mrs. Walter Stuhr, Mrs. Thomas Amberg.

Appendices

Officers and Directors of Madonna Center, 1913-1964

Laurance Acker
Mary Agnes Amberg
Thomas H. Amberg
William A. Amberg
Mrs. William A. Amberg
Mrs. Lester Armour
Mrs. James E. Baggot, Jr.
Mrs. James H. Barnard
Thomas H. Beacom
Thomas H. Beacom, Jr.
James M. Bennan
Robert L. Berner, Jr.
Joseph F. Bigane, Sr.
William J. Bogan
Mrs. Malcolm J. Boyle
Mrs. Frank M. Breen, Jr.
Mrs. John M. Breen, Jr.
David F. Bremner
Mrs. David F. Bremner
James V. Bremner
Amy Brewer
Mrs. John H. Burgee
Mrs. William F. Cagney
Frank M. Callahan
Otto M. Carry
Otto M. Carry, Jr.
Mrs. Joseph J. Cavanagh
Beth Coleman
Thomas J. Condon
Mrs. Frank A. Connolly, Jr.
William J. Corbett
Mrs. John D. Crawford
Joseph W. Cremin

William A. Cremin
Mark A. Cronin, Jr.
John V. Crowe, Jr.
Mary T. Cudahy
Hon. Walter J. Cummings
Walter J. Cummings, Jr.
Richmond Dean
Thomas A. Dean
Thomas F. Delaney
Mrs. Thomas C. Dennehy
Dr. Alfred DeRoulet
Matthew Dillon
James J. Doheny
Mrs. James J. Doheny
Mrs. James P. Dolan
Mrs. George F. Douaire, Jr.
Mrs. Harry L. Drake
George P. Ducharme
Neil P. Dungan
Patricia Dunn
Robert A. Dwyer
Barbara Farley
Peter V. Fazio
Albert C. Fellinger, Jr.
Mrs. John J. Flanagan
Joanna Fortune
Msgr. E. J. Fox
Virginia L. Fox
John J. Gaskell
Gretchen Gastreich
John Gerlach
Mary Jane Gerrity
Angela Gillespie

214

Frank J. Gillespie, Jr.
Mrs. George P. Gilman
Richard P. Ginder
Dr. John F. Golden
Mrs. John F. Golden
Mrs. John W. Goldthwaite, Jr.
Mrs. Frank M. Gordon
Thomas R. Graham
Patrick A. Grogan
Mrs. John T. Groth
Mrs. Thomas Hallinan
Mrs. Robert Harmon
James Hayes
Audrey Heinemann
Matthew J. Hickey, III
Adelia Hopkins
Mrs. Edward N. Hurley, Jr.
Mrs. Michael J. Igoe
Leontine Inderrieden
Malcolm F. Johnson
Mrs. Malcolm F. Johnson
Mrs. Leith Johnston
Mrs. Michael V. Kannally
Hutchins D. Kealy
Marilyn Keeley
Mrs. Kent Kelley
Mrs. Edward P. Kelly
Hon. Martin H. Kennelly
Charles Kerwin
Edward M. Kerwin
Mrs. Edward J. Lawler
Russell J. Leander
Robert B. Liepold
Thomas J. Lyman
Dwight McKay
Dr. George W. Mahoney
Mrs. George W. Mahoney
Louis F. Mahoney, Jr.
Judy Masterman
Elmer J. Mercil
Mrs. Stella Metzger Mercil
Francis J. Milligan, Jr.

Mrs. Ralph J. Mills
Mrs. Edward Mooney
Simon J. Morand, III
Bette Mulholland
Paul L. Mullaney
George J. Murphy
Mary Camille Murray
Mrs. Frances J. Noonan
Mrs. Edward O'Callaghan
Dr. John B. O'Donoghue, Jr.
John F. O'Keefe
Mrs. Edwin H. O'Mara
Mrs. James R. O'Riley
Mary K. O'Sullivan
Edwin H. Omara
Mrs. Edwin H. Omara
Edmund J. Orr
Stuyvesant Peabody
Stuyvesant Peabody, Jr.
George L. Plamondon, Jr.
Harold M. Plamondon
Marie Plamondon
June Adele Rettig
Mrs. Allen B. Ripley
Catherine A. Rogers
Mrs. Martin J. Russell
Mrs. Henry L. Sanderson
Mrs. Otto F. G. Schilling
Mrs. J. Donald Scott
Rev. F. Siedenburg, S.J.
Sherman J. Sexton
Mrs. Albert P. Smola
Mrs. Charles F. Spalding
Mrs. William A. Spencer
Frank R. Stenson
Alfred C. Stepan, Jr.
Walter A. Stuhr, Jr.
Mrs. Bolton Sullivan
Dr. Richard J. Tivnen
Richard A. Walsh
Mortimer C. Watters
James J. White

Officers and Directors of
The Associates of Madonna Center

216

Audrey Heinemann
Matthew J. Hickey, III
Mrs. William E. Hovan
Hutchins D. Kealy
Marilyn Keeley
Mrs. Kent Kelley
Mrs. Kip Kelley
Mrs. Edward P. Kelly
Catherine Kenny
Kathryn Kerwin
Mrs. Thomas J. Kerwin
Mrs. Robert B. Liepold
George C. Lyman, Jr.
Louise Lyman
Thomas J. Lyman
Mrs. Fred M. McCahey
Jerome C. McCarthy
Rita McCarthy
James P. McCourt
Mrs. James P. McCourt
Mary McDonough
L. Carle McEvoy, Jr.
John C. McGuinn
Mrs. John A. McGuire
Mrs. Walter McGuire, Jr.
Mrs. Donald P. McIntyre
Dwight McKay
Mrs. William P. McKeever
William G. Mahon
Mrs. Louis F. Mahoney, Jr.
Judy Masterman
Francis J. Milligan, Jr.
Mrs. Edward Mooney
Simon J. Morand, III
Bette Mulholland
Mrs. Charles Murphy, Jr.
George J. Murphy
Mrs. William J. Murphy
Mary Camille Murray
Noel Nelson
William F. O'Connor
John O'Dea

Rosemary O'Neil
Thomas E. O'Neill
Mrs. James R. O'Riley
Mary Kay O'Sullivan
Robert Oakley
Edmund J. Orr
B. Michael Pallasch
Stuyvesant Peabody
George L. Plamondon, Jr.
Harold M. Plamondon
Marie Plamondon
Joan Potter
John P. Quinlan
William E. Rach
Thomas W. Reilly
June Adele Rettig
Mrs. Thomas A. Reynolds, Jr.
Frederick Riley
James Riley
Mrs. Robert F. Riley
Catherine Rogers
Frank J. Rothing
Mrs. Frank J. Rothing
Daniel Ryan, Jr.
Mrs. Donald R. Ryan
Mrs. Henry L. Sanderson
Joan Schlessinger
Mrs. Jesse M. Shaver, Jr.
Donald Sheridan
Mrs. Albert P. Smola
Robert Snediker
William A. Spencer
Mrs. William A. Spencer
Mrs. William E. Sterling
Walter A. Stuhr, Jr.
Harold E. Sullivan
Mrs. Harold W. Sullivan
Richard A. Walsh
Mrs. Richard D. Wehman
James J. White
Margery Wild
Janet Williams
Adam Wolf

Officers and Directors of
The Christ-Child Society, Chicago, 1907-1975

Mrs. Bertrand I. Amberg
Mary Agnes Amberg
Mrs. Thomas H. Amberg
Mrs. Lester Armour
Mrs. Stanton Armour
Mrs. James E. Baggot, Jr.
Mrs. Thomas H. Beacom
Mrs. John Caspar Bick
Mary Kathryn Bick
Mrs. Stephen E. Boback
Mrs. John J. Bowen, Jr.
Mrs. John J. Bowen, III
Mrs. Malcolm J. Boyle
Mrs. Ray A. Braddock
Mrs. Edward G. Bremner
Mrs. James G. Brennan
Mrs. Britton I. Budd
Mrs. Ivo W. Buddeke
Mrs. John Russell Burdick
Mrs. Charles T. Byrne
Mrs. Jane L. Caestecker
Mrs. Julien J. Caestecker
Mrs. Francis M. Callahan
Mrs. Eugene J. Carroll
Mrs. Martin C. Carroll
Mrs. Joseph J. Cavanagh
Mrs. Richard A. Cavenaugh
Mrs. John Walter Clarke
Mrs. Frederic J. Clifford
Mrs. John Coleman
Mrs. Thomas J. Condon
Mrs. George J. Cooke
Mrs. Albert R. Copeland
Mrs. William J. Corbett
Mrs. Edward D. Corboy
Mrs. Eugene F. Corcoran
Mrs. Leo P. Corcoran
William A. Cremin
Mrs. William A. Cremin
Mrs. Edward M. Cummings
Mrs. Leo P. Cummings
Mrs. Walter J. Cummings
Mrs. Michael J. Cunningham

Mrs. Thomas A. Dean
Mrs. John F. Detmer
Mrs. James P. Dolan
Mrs. William G. Dooley
Mrs. Querin P. Dorschel
Mrs. Daniel L. Douaire
Mrs. Harry L. Drake
Mrs. Robert Jerome Dunne
Mrs. Robert E. Fanning
Mrs. Peter V. Fazio
Mrs. George Fiedler
Mrs. J. Paul Fogarty
Mrs. John L. Fortune
Mrs. Thomas Frank Geraghty
Mrs. Norman H. Gerlach
Mrs. Marah M. Goes
Mrs. Frank M. Gordon
Mrs. Gilbert S. Haggerty
Mrs. Martin J. Harding
Mrs. John P. Henebry
Mrs. John W. Hughes
Mrs. Edward N. Hurley, Jr.
Mrs. Michael L. Igoe, Jr.
Mrs. Malcolm F. Johnson
Mrs. D. F. Kelly
Mrs. John E. Kenny
Mrs. Edward M. Kerwin
Mrs. John Kinsella
Mrs. William R. Kohl
Mrs. John J. Krez
Mrs. Garrett F. Larkin
Mary Frances Lavezzorio
Mrs. Nicholas J. Lavezzorio
Katherine K. Lawler
Mrs. William J. Lawlor, Jr.
Mrs. John K. Leander
Mrs. Arthur T. Leonard
Mrs. Edward K. MacDonald
Mrs. James B. McCahey
Mrs. Robert N. McCreary
Mrs. Charles L. McEvoy
Mrs. Michael F. McGuire
Mrs. H. S. McKinley

Mrs. George McLaughlin
Mrs. James F. McNulty, Jr.
Mrs. William B. McNulty
Mrs. Alfred W. Mansfield
Mrs. Charles H. Moody
Mrs. Simon J. Morand
Mrs. Henry C. Murphy
Mrs. James D. Murphy
Mrs. John L. Nelson
Mrs. William F. O'Connor
Mrs. Vincent J. O'Conor
Rosemary O'Neil
Mrs. Joseph J. O'Shaughnessy
Mrs. Stuyvesant Peabody
Marie Plamondon
Mrs. Lefens Porter
Mrs. Philip J. Reddy
Mrs. James P. Reichmann
Mrs. Don H. Reuben
Mrs. R. Joseph Rich

Mrs. John C. Rodkey
Mrs. Frank J. Rothing
Mrs. Charles J. Roubik
Mrs. Ralph G. Ryan, Jr.
Mrs. William A. Ryan
Mrs. James A. Sackley
Mrs. Raben C. Schenk
Mrs. J. Donald Scott
Mrs. T. Mackin Sexton
Mrs. William C. Sexton
Mrs. William P. Smyth
Mrs. Charles F. Spalding
Mrs. Walter A. Stuhr, Jr.
Mrs. Bolton Sullivan
Mrs. Quintin S. Sykes
Mrs. William Templeton
Mrs. Reuben Thorson
Mrs. Harold G. Ward
Mrs. Hempstead Washburne
Mrs. Oliver A. Williams
Mrs. Quinn Wold

Staff Members of Madonna Center

Mrs. Camille Amato
Elizabeth Amberg
Mary Agnes Amberg
Mary Audeuk
Mrs. F. J. Budinger
Cecilia Burns
Demetria Castro
Alice C. Coleman
Cecille Courtney
Helen Courtney
Margaret Curran
Louis Davino
Gina DelBoccio
Joseph Diggles
Mrs. James Doheny
Sam Esposito
Mrs. Mary Franklin
Anastasia Furlong
Diane Gentile
Richard Gonzalez
Mrs. Carmen Gradi
Irving Halbeck
Robert Halbeck
Marie Hammill
Mrs. Jennie Iozzo
Mrs. Helen Jank
John Jasinski
Catherine Jordan
Louise Kirch
Eulalia Koller
Catherine Lane
Michael Libero
Anthony Lymperis
Mrs. Sally McMahon
Marguerite McManemin
Mary Louise McPartlin
Marian Madigan
Mary Meade

Anthony Mentone
Donald Mentone
Frank Mentone
Peter Mentone
Mrs. James P. Morley
Mrs. Edith Napolitano
Nell O'Brien
Catherine O'Connor
Mrs. Edwin Omara
Shirley Omara
Camille Onesto
Michael Onesto
Mary K. O'Sullivan
Margaret Payne
Mrs. Augusta Perry
Antoinette Pintozzi
Josephine Pintozzi
Lucille Pintozzi
Mary Pintozzi
Marie Plamondon
Millie Richards
Marjorie Riley
Mrs. J. Rodkey
Gwen Sanderson
Edward Scaccia
Mrs. Otto Schilling
Mrs. Violet Schoebel
Mary Sennott
Mrs. James Stanley Smith
Robert S. Terry
William Tozzi
Joseph Vece
Mickelyn Vece
William Vespo
Mrs. Florence Vestuto
Florence Wagner
Winifred Willis
Ann Wimmer
Doris Ann Wright

The manuscript for this book was completed in 1942. It's publication at this time in this form owes much to the help of the following people.

Judge and Mrs. George Fiedler, Mrs. Mary Candice, and Nell O'Brien for many photographs and much valuable information.

Thomas Graham, last president of the Madonna Center Associate Group, gave valuable assistance, as did Mrs. Kay Rodkey, secretary of the Christ-Child Society.

Mary Ann Johnson, administrator of Jane Addams Hull-House, provided the photos which appear on pages 35, 37, 84, 191, and 195; courtesy University of Illinois Library at Chicago Circle Campus, Jane Addams Memorial Collection.

We are also indebted to Mary Louise McPartlin, Katherine Bogan, Sr. Patricia Vaira, O.S.F., Mary Garramone, and John Triss, graphics curator of the Chicago Historical Society, for photographs.

We also received help from Paul Gratke, archivist, Marquette University Library, Becky Sutton, Chicago Archdiocesan Information Office, Mrs. F. Williams, reference librarian, Chicago Board of Education, Debbie Morrow, Chicago Municipal Reference Library, and Richard O. Walsh.

The neighborhood clergy supplied us with factual information; Rev. David McCarthy, S.J., Holy Family Church; Rev. Angelo Calandra, C.S., Our Lady of Pompeii; Rev. Tom Paramo, C.M.F., St. Francis of Assisi, and Rev. Salvatore DeVita, C.S.

The book also owes much to the staff of Loyola
University Press, especially Rev. Vincent C. Hor-
rigan, director, Marian McCann and Helen Faul.

George A. Lane, S.J.
August 1976